For Etjenne

Martin Hendel

The Good Production Planner

A Business Novel

How to Get the Right Mindset and
an Aligned Supply Chain to
Become a Successful
Supply Chain Manager

Legal Notice

Covered events and people are fictional and any resemblance to person living or dead is purely coincidental.

Based on: (UN)PLANBAR

Translation: Martin Hendel

Cover design: Aksaramantra

Proofreading & Editing: Melissa Prideaux

Contact: martin@deine-lieferkette.de

Erzbergerstr. 33

78224 Singen

Germany

ISBN: 9798820061301

Independently published

CONTENTS

1 - The Job Offer

The alarm clock rings. I turn to see what time it is. It's 4:30 a.m. I'm tired and don't want to get up - my head full of thoughts, it took me far too long to fall asleep again last night. For months now, I've had to wake up this early on Monday mornings as my current job requires me to travel around Europe.

I get out of bed, give my girlfriend Sophia a kiss and take a shower. My morning routine gets going and after thirty minutes, I'm ready to go. My suitcase and backpack are packed as usual. I usually pack enough to get me through to Thursday evening. Before I leave our flat in Schaffhausen, I write a small note and tape it to the flat entrance door. Dozens of other notes are already hanging there. From a distance, the door no longer looks like wood, but like it's freshly wallpapered. I feel guilty about being away all week, so writing notes is a kind of routine and a lovely greeting. Today I find it particularly difficult to find nice words, as we had an argument last night. I notice that I'm often unbalanced and my stress-level increases on Sundays before the new working week. I like my life, but I'm dissatisfied because I'm less and less autonomous. At least, that's what I'm imagining at the moment. The note says:

To the world, you are just anyone. But to me, you are the world. I'm sorry. Have a nice week. Kisses, Gabriel

That's pretty cheesy, I know. But it's also part of my personality.

I close the door and walk to the underground car-park where my car is parked. On the drive to Zurich airport, I can hardly wait to catch up on some sleep on the plane.

Fortunately, we have rented various company parking spaces at the airport, so I don't have to look for one and I gain time. I usually arrive at the last minute. To my surprise, I haven't missed a single flight in over a hundred a year – even when I got stuck in the airport lift for about ten minutes a few weeks ago.

I park the car and walk towards the departure hall. On one of the countless monitors, I search for the 6:40 a.m. flight to Amsterdam, flight number *KL 1952*. After locating the gate, I pass the security check – I'm already checked in and only have hand luggage. Finally, I board the plane with KLM printed in blue capital letters on the tail. After stowing my luggage and taking my seat, I fall asleep and only wake up to the shaking of the plane as it touches the runway at Schiphol, Amsterdam. I leave the airport by train to Rotterdam. I like these yellow and blue double-decker trains. On the train I start working, read various e-mails and make some preparations for the day. In Rotterdam, I take a taxi towards the factory, which is near the stadium of the local football club, Feyenoord Rotterdam.

I've been visiting the Netherlands regularly for a few years now and I really like Rotterdam. Growing up in a small German town with just seven thousand inhabitants, I like the cosmopolitanism and the hustle and bustle of this city. The factory is right on the waterfront and the national headquarters of my employer in the Netherlands towers above it. The countless offices of the bridge-like building float majestically above the historic production halls.

I take the less luxurious entrance and walk quickly along the production halls, choose the large gate through which forklifts move in and out, and enter our open-plan office. The office is rather rudimentarily furnished, like many workplaces at a production site, less glamorous when I compare this with the modern open spaces of the head office. I don't mind because the people I share the space with make all the difference. After a nice greeting and small talk about our weekends, I get down to work.

We are one of the largest margarine factories in the world. For six months now, I've been temporarily in charge of the site's supply chain management. After I spent more than a year supervising two production sites in the Netherlands, introducing new company processes and implementing a new production planning software solution, I was asked to take over the management of the plant's supply chain in addition to the project. I received this request overnight when a surprising personnel decision was made regarding my predecessor. I didn't have to think twice as at the age of twenty-four, this was a great opportunity for me. Nevertheless, the position is only meant to be temporary, as Sophia won't agree to move to the Netherlands. I still feel a little melancholy thinking about giving up this role soon. I've enjoyed being responsible for logistics, production planning, procurement of components and, above all, the team. It fills me with joy to tackle the many challenges, learn something new every day and celebrate small successes with my colleagues.

When I switch on my notebook, an e-mail from Pieter Smith catches my eye. The content is brief with a request for a phone call. Pieter is one of my biggest personal challenges, but at the same time a strong supporter of my development. Without hesitation, I pick up the phone and dial his number. He picks up, greets me with his Flemish accent and teasingly asks me why I took so long to call. Pieter has mastered the game of putting light pressure on his counterparts. It's a kind of fun but, at the same time, a test to see how quick-witted you are in your response.

I like to remember my job interview two years ago. My first visit to Rotterdam. I was excited, especially because I'd had little contact with people from higher management levels. Pieter picked me up at the gate that day and I immediately thought of

"Doc", Dr. Emmett Brown from the movie *Back to the Future,* when Pieter introduced himself. It was a cold day and his long coat and grey hair fluttered in the wind. He grinned mischievously and I noticed the mixture of cheeky childishness and hardened businessman. I estimated he was in his late fifties.

On the way to the temporary container offices, he smoked a cigar and we made small talk. At that time, smoking was still allowed in some places on the premises. He put me through the wringer because I wasn't wearing a tie with my suit. He was serious and only let up after I was able to give a reasonable explanation. The content of the explanation was less important to him than how I handled the small pressure situation. Over time, I've noticed these little tests again and again. He also uses them with other colleagues, but I imagine that he's particularly eager to do so for those employees in whom he sees some potential.

Back to the phone call. Pieter gets straight to the point.

"Gabriel, we have an issue in our Czech plant, near Prague, and I want you to complete the management team of this site as an expatriate. Basically, we're dissatisfied with the performance of the current customer service & logistics manager. You will work for him for the time being, but in the medium term I want you to take over from him. We're currently investing a lot of money in the site, in new production lines and technologies, but the external perception and delivery performance are very poor and urgently need to be improved."

I interrupt him. "Ok, thanks for the vote of confidence, but could I please think about it and get more details?"

"Yes, please call Mike Pence, he can give you some background and details. But I'd like to have your response tomorrow morning. You need to be in Prague as early as next month to start your onboarding."

We end the phone call. I'm confused. A mixture of euphoria and uncertainty spreads through me. I'm on autopilot for the rest of the working day, as I can't sort out my thoughts properly.

I call Mike. He's a good work colleague from our supply chain headquarters and takes care of the central planning of the global network of factories and suppliers. We've known each other for more than two years and have implemented various projects together. I'm sure that he will give an objective but also honest assessment of the initial situation and challenges of the plant in the Czech Republic. I'm surprised that his response doesn't scare me off but rather arouses curiosity and a certain ambition in me. Fragments of the conversation remain with me, such as "unreliable, poor forecasts, insufficiently qualified employees, high fluctuation, worst customer service in the network, many projects and new products, simply unplannable".

After work, I regularly walk for kilometres in the dark through the city streets towards my hotel. Rotterdam's bridges fascinate me. I cross the Erasmus Bridge on foot in the evening. It has two dominant metre-high columns and, in one direction, a multitude of mighty steel cables stretching out like a classical fan. To the left and right, skyscrapers rise and the lights in the windows illuminate the night sky.

Today I have a lot to process and think about, which is why I take various detours so that I only arrive at the hotel ninety minutes later. Check-in goes smoothly, as always. I'm almost part of the inventory of this hotel; most of the staff know me and call me by name. Once in my room, I call Sophia and tell her the news – the second offer I've received for a key management job within a very short time. This time I probably won't be able to say no.

2 - Welcome to Nelahozeves

A few weeks later, I'm at Prague airport waiting for my ride. The night was even shorter than usual. I kept waking up, feeling a mixture of nervousness and excitement. As a result, my body is getting into gear slowly and my stomach is sensitive. Whenever I feel nervous, it hits my stomach. In today's case, however, my nervousness shouldn't be negative because I'm looking forward to the assignment and have consciously decided to do this. Our bodies and minds like to play tricks on us in such circumstances and make us react similarly to both positive and negative events. I concentrate on my breathing and quickly get back into balance.

A friendly-looking older gentleman comes running into the airport reception hall with a sign stating "Gabriel Wolf". I walk up to him, and he introduces himself as Marek. A little later we're sitting in his light blue Ford Mondeo and drive about forty minutes to the production plant north of Prague. With every kilometre away from Prague, I feel like we're travelling back in time. The towns and villages seem from another, simpler era. The ride is entertaining, as Marek tries to give me a lot of information in his mixture of broken English and German. He is immediately likeable, down-to-earth, marked by a life full of work but friendly and warm-hearted. His company makes me feel less nervous.

We reach our destination, Nelahozeves, a small village with just over two thousand inhabitants. The village is on the Vltava river and has just two sights, a castle and the birthplace of the composer Antonín Dvořák. I didn't realise before that the town was home to only three times as many citizens as my new workplace, a factory with over seven hundred employees.

We pass the factory security and drive onto the premises. As I get out of the car, I'm impressed by the sheer size of the site. There are various building complexes housing offices, in addition to various production technologies and even a food oil refinery, several warehouses, a factory-owned locomotive standing on the tracks next to countless tall metal tanks, and several forklifts and trucks driving across the site. Marek takes me to the administration building and points to a display case showing the factory management. There's already a picture of me with the title "Head of Planning & Materials Management".

I should be bursting with pride, but I'm overcome by a sense of humility. I'm only in my mid-twenties. I feel what a great responsibility it is to be part of this small management team in charge of shaping the future of this factory, which has such a long tradition and so many employees. Nevertheless, my excitement at the challenges ahead prevails.

Thoughts of pivotal moments flash through my mind. I think about when I left home at the age of sixteen to do an apprenticeship. Because I was underage, I had to live as a subtenant with an unknown family hundreds of kilometres away from home. I remember the countless hours I spent in a truck every week driving home for the weekend because I had no money for a train ticket.

I completed the Logistics Management Certificate and then the Business Administration Certificate part-time in order to have more knowledge about certain management theory. Admittedly, I haven't had any time at all during the last few years to enjoy my progress, personal development or success. Now here I am, in the Czech Republic, about to take on my first long-term position and major responsibility, opening another chapter again, without reflection or pause.

I'm given a friendly reception. After a conversation with the HR and plant manager, I get to know my team, or more precisely, the team leaders who will report directly to me. When I see that the four junior managers are excited, I feel a little more confident - shared pain is half the pain. I grin broadly and say "*Dobrý den, jmenuji se Gabriel*". My pronunciation is so bad it immediately breaks the ice because they all start to laugh. I always find these first touch points to be a key experience. After all, I'll spend a lot of my time with these people.

Jana is standing directly in front of me. I guess she's a bit older than me. Compared to my height of one hundred and seventy-three metres, she is tall, athletic and has long blonde hair. Jana takes care of project management like new product launches. Since she's a former management trainee, she knows all the departments at the site. My impression of her is that she is quick-witted but also trustworthy.

The person next to her introduces herself to me as Magdalena. She tells me directly about her little daughter, whom she is bringing up alone, so she has to leave work early, though she usually continues working from home in the evenings. Magdalena comes across as tough and strong-willed, at least that's what I imagine from her sporty figure and short black hair. She leads the group of production and material planners in the production unit for salad dressings, ketchup and mayonnaise.

The next of my new colleagues, Ondrej, seems short-tempered or not very communicative. I estimate he's in his mid-thirties. He has a strong handshake, and later I discover that this may come from his regular climbing tours. Ondrej has been in the department the longest and is responsible for the production and material planning of the margarine production as well as the vitamin shots production, which has recently been started up.

Jakub, who is tall and looks to be in my age group, brings up the rear. He seems to be quite humorous and makes our newly formed group laugh again. He oversees transport planning and export administration to the more than twenty countries that are supplied from the storage locations of the factory.

My colleagues accompany me to my new office, which is right next to the open-plan office of my new department and is equipped with a large modern desk, a meeting table and the necessary IT equipment. It's been a while since I've had my own office. And it won't stay that way for long because in the next few weeks, I'll have part of the wall removed in order to have a direct connection to my team's open-plan office. It's important for me to absorb the atmosphere and mood of the team, to feel the rhythm of the hustle and bustle, but also to be visible and tangible myself. Since I've been a leader, I've become aware of how quickly you can lose touch with the team as you run from appointment to appointment and spend your few spare moments at your desk, silent and invisible. I feel that the personal touch, sharing emotions and being a role model, especially for young and dynamic groups, is vital. Even though I may be the supervisor, I'm part of the team and its dynamics, the successes as well as the failures. If someone needs to discuss something confidential or personal, we can use a meeting room or even go for a walk.

Towards the end of the day comes the hardest part. There's a knock at my office door and a strong man with the hairstyle and charisma of a military officer enters the room. His name is Vladimir Horak, and as of today, he has to cede some of his responsibilities to me. From now on, he is only responsible for the physical part of logistics, that is, storage and transport. At least on paper. In the team itself, he will continue to act as an informal superior in the coming weeks and this will present me with some challenges. What depresses me when we first meet is that I've already been informed that he will have to leave his position in the medium term so that I can take over the complete logistics function. This makes me feel permanently guilty, because Vladimir, apart from his professional problems, is right-hearted, works hard and acts responsibly.

Several times over the next weeks, Vladimir will prove his skills and knowledge in logistics, and I'll learn a lot from him in this respect. But the growing demands on supply chain management, the interaction of all functions along the supply chain from the supplier to the customer, have placed new demands on him that some of the managers at the head office no longer trust him with. This will not be the first or last time I have a hidden agenda at this location.

Tomorrow I'll meet the rest of the management team. I'm especially curious about the production leader because, from experience, this is where there is the greatest potential for conflict concerning our improvement measures. I recall an argument with the production manager in Rotterdam. We got into such a tiff that I asked her to leave the office immediately in front of the whole team. A few hours later, of course, we resolved our argument, although we never agreed on the issue of "efficiency versus production agility".

It's been dark for a while, and it's already after 7:00 in the evening. Marek drives me back to Prague where I'll stay at the Hilton Hotel on the outskirts of the city. This huge and luxurious cuboid will be my weekly residence for the next while, at least until I can move with Sophia into a permanent home.

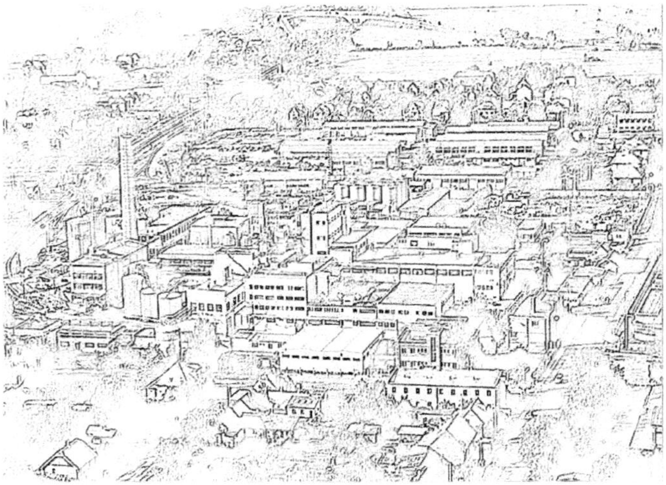

3 - Getting to Know the Team

In the first month, above all, I want to observe: to understand the skills and motivation of my team, to build a network across the different local departments and to identify the reasons for non-performance and the required improvement measures.

I find it difficult to hold back obvious quick wins. Due to my past project assignments, I've got to know many production sites and supply chain areas. As a result, I imagine that I have found an optimal structure and process chain. But I also want to allow local nuances or peculiarities to remain intact because otherwise you lose the team or the organisation during the process of change. It is not very easy to convey to long-term employees that everything was done wrong in the past. This is, of course, not the case. Furthermore, not every concept will be able to deliver one hundred per cent the same results if local conditions are not taken into account. Often undertakings with the best intentions do not deliver desired results, and the team builds little trust - with comments like "he thinks he knows everything better, anyway," "he doesn't listen to us," or "he's not interested in other approaches". I firmly believe that you can learn something everywhere - every person, every organisation has abilities that you can learn from – you just have to look closely, get involved and, above all, listen to your teams or peers.

I can divide my young and dynamic team into three groups. In the first group, I recognise a high potential with diverse skills or talents. The second group consists of hard-working team members who do their work well and with pleasure, but probably have lower potential. The remaining staff I should get to know better to understand whether they lack the motivation, the will to change or the skills to cope better with the assigned tasks.

At the beginning, I concentrate primarily on the first group, because this is where the time invested will yield the greatest return; at best, these are also people who are in a direct reporting line to the supervisor and who themselves lead employees. The goal is to create real lighthouses through coaching-like conversations and knowledge transfer. After a while, these team members should have a positive halo effect on their surroundings, peers and colleagues, demonstrating the need for change or supporting it, and providing orientation to the team. In this way, the supervisor is not permanently in the spotlight and, over time, a jointly formulated and presented programme emerges.

Pieter gave me a tip before I started the position. I should choose a trusted person in the team with whom I can talk about everything - exchange thoughts, test suggestions for change. Through such exchange, I can get valuable tips on the team and also receive open feedback on my suggestions or my behaviour - thus, feedback for personal development. Along the way, you build up a reliable "right hand", whom you can trust blindly, and a potential successor. Pretty soon it's clear to me that Jana, with her enthusiastic, interested, down-to-earth and eager nature, could be that person. She has a positive world view - one of the most important qualities in my opinion. Having loads of naysayers in a team is like poison and will cause a lot of frustration in the long run. Above all, the fun factor at work may get lost.

Something I observe and would like to put an end to quickly is that Vladimir spends a lot of time with our staff. Having a closer look, I see his strong desire to enforce direct control, thus allowing little room for personal experience. Examples of this are the daily telephone conferences with colleagues like Mike from our head office or also the internal customers from the international sales companies. Vladimir does not trust the production planners to make independent arrangements or to provide information about relevant events. I can understand his actions because employees like Leos are very young and inexperienced. But in the medium term, he is downgrading individual members to assistants instead of allowing them to make autonomous decisions or come up with their own suggestions. It goes without saying that the motivation of the people concerned is impacted. I know this from my own experience: Whenever I'm on the "long leash" and can celebrate successes as well as experience failures by myself, I automatically find many potential solutions to the issues at stake and ask for feedback or timely support. As a leader, I have a positive perception of people and believe that the vast majority want to do a good job. I imagine that without this positive view of people, leaders will not be successful in the long run or at least negatively influence their environment.

In the back of my mind, I have Pieter's "command and control" approach. He always does well with this in crisis management, centralises decisions and leaves little room for negative outbursts in the organisation. I have seen this in action many times and cannot deny its success. However, I'm in this factory to create a change and a kind of turnaround – not to constantly survive by short-term firefighting and possibly damaging any basic good already in place. At least, I don't see myself as a crisis manager. In my career, I want to be perceived as a doer and, above all, a coach – to lead via fun and advice instead of pressure. Ultimately, as leaders, we have to remain agile and adapt our style slightly depending on the situation – without appearing inauthentic. The latter would be very exhausting in the long run.

After a few days, I grab Leos for a one-on-one. I ask him how he likes it here at the factory and what he's learned in the last few months. He is only twenty years old and in his very first job he has the responsibility of planning the production of one of the site's emerging production technologies. I should say, in my view, planning is the heartbeat of the supply chain. This is where sales requirements are converted into target stocks, procurement, transport volumes or production orders. Leos's work thus has a significant impact on costs or the service level of the site.

We have a good conversation

"I'm very grateful for the opportunity I've been given with this job," Leos tells me. "My father has worked in production at this factory for over twenty-five years. I'm from here, I live just a few houses away and I want to contribute to the plant's development."

It almost sounds like a rehearsed sentence during a job interview, but I sense how sincere he is in this statement.

"Tell me, if your father works in production, how familiar are you with our production facilities, but also the team on-site?"

"Very. I'm over on the shop floor every day. I have a good relationship with the operators and the head of production. By the way, I think some of our service problems are triggered because of volume fluctuations in production output. But even my father thinks this can't be because our efficiency is good, at least on most lines."

I perk up my ears, probe a little further and then ask Leos to run some analyses over the next days.

Then I change the subject. "What's your understanding of the role of a production planner and do you have the impression that you're carrying out this role?"

"Well, I make sure that our customers have sufficient stock cover in their local storage locations and that the production is utilised to achieve target efficiencies. To be honest, though, I don't feel like I'm doing my job properly. I'm constantly preparing evaluations and commenting on where and why we are having stock availability problems again. I'm always dealing with the past and Vladimir is always dictating to me what I should or shouldn't do. I can't present some of my ideas and I don't even dare to ask for help because we don't have time to breathe and think because of all the escalations. I also have the feeling that I don't do my work well and learn little myself. No one takes the time to explain various approaches to me, I'm just bombarded with constant instructions and there's so much pressure. I'm sorry, I'm moaning now – I know we need to improve."

"There's nothing to be sorry about. I expect us to be honest with each other and express our feelings. That's the only way we can build mutual understanding. It's only grumbling if you don't give a reason for your dissatisfaction or don't provide alternatives!"

Here, too, an initial suspicion is confirmed about something that I could perceive almost everywhere in my project role. The planning horizon is too short-term focused, the more hectic the situation, the more weight is given to the tangible, obvious weeks or months. The understanding of roles, or rather the division of the individual supply chain tasks, is not distinctive or differentiated enough and thus there are no real experts or coordinated process flows. To put it boldly, one could say: everyone does a little bit of everything.

As far as Leos is concerned, I have a good feeling and suggest that we now sit down together regularly to share our knowledge or to deepen it together.

I'm not so sure about other colleagues. Ondrej, for example, appears very confident and can answer many of my questions satisfactorily. I also notice that Vladimir gives him much more space and thus confidence. In fact, the key performance indicators, especially customer service for his area of responsibility, don't seem to be doing too badly at all. But I get quite sceptical feedback from Ondrej when I ask questions, especially when I want to get more insight into details. Unfortunately, I also get statements to which I react allergically, such as, "We've always done it this way" or "This has been agreed with Pavel and production, so we don't need to carry out another analysis here".

I increasingly have the impression that Ondrej as a leader does not involve his team enough and thus seems indispensable. I'll have to resolve this by getting into one-to-one discussions with his team to better understand the dynamics and his influence.

In terms of building a local network of colleagues, I'm making good progress. The leadership team is open-minded toward me and since we speak fluent English with each other, there is at least no language barrier here. In my own team, communication also works well; only a few of my colleagues are a bit reserved or at least not comfortable speaking in a foreign language, even about personal things at lunch or small talk in the corridor. I'm usually a quick learner, but languages are unfortunately not one of my strengths. Therefore, apart from the usual pleasantries such as "*Dobrý den*" for "Good day", "*Hezký večer*" for "Have a nice evening" or "*Hezký víkend*" for "I wish you a nice weekend", I hardly get any words in Czech past my lips.

Our plant controller, Martin, is an interesting character. At first glance he seems a bit special – with his long hair tied in a braid and his reserved manner. But once the ice is broken, he's great to talk to. His long hair is also quickly explained as soon as he talks about his hobby, playing drums in a heavy metal band. From his behaviour, I wouldn't have thought so, but it doesn't make his facets any less diverse. Since my focus is supply chain planning and control, we understand each other right away. We're both interested in numbers, data and facts and try to bring transparency into the factory's processes. Furthermore, Martin is very meticulous and always has some overview or database ready for my various questions. Over the years, he has accumulated an immense amount of knowledge that I, as a newcomer, am only too happy to tap into.

My worry about getting to know the production manager was unfounded. Pavel, like so many of his peers, is overly focused on optimising costs and increasing efficiency. But his open-minded, dynamic and likeable manner makes him easy to approach and gives me an expandable basis for the projects to come. Nothing is worse than working in silos at one location with little willingness to compromise.

In the latest management meeting, Martin presents a simple model on this topic, which he calls the "golden triangle of our factory". He grabs the flipchart and a thick felt-tip pen and draws a large triangle in the middle of the sheet. At the top he writes "customer service" and describes it as synonymous with the revenue we can generate from the products we make. At the bottom right corner, he writes down "costs" and gives examples such as manufacturing costs, procurement costs of raw materials or packaging materials, storage and transport costs. He labels the third corner "capital". His examples this time are tied-up capital in the form of stocks or investments in new production facilities.

He now takes a red pen and writes down two equations:

Revenue - Costs = Profit

Profit / Capital Employed = Return On Capital Employed (ROCE)

We then discuss various ways to impact the "golden triangle". For example, we could generate additional income through extended flexibility, such as reactive capacities for short-term demand requests from our sales organisations. The profit should increase to the extent that the extra income generated exceeds the costs incurred to maintain the additional capacities required. Moreover, if we do not have to build up significantly higher inventories in the form of components or semi-finished products or invest in additional capabilities for our production lines, a better operating result will ultimately be generated. If we eliminate products and thus capacities that yield only low or little margins we will also increase our ROCE. Thus, the cost savings or even capital reductions could also lead to a better operating result. Martin then sends me a link to the book *The Strategy-Driven Supply Chain* by Bram DeSmet so I can dig deeper into the topic.

After this talk, we move swiftly to the topic of goal setting. As leaders, we have a significant portion of our annual income tied to an agreed-upon goal achievement. Goal setting is a balancing act. At one end of the continuum is the departmental or division-specific goal such as high production efficiency or low-cost structure. At the opposite end is a community goal such as high customer service. The first example is easy to delineate, but often increasingly triggers a conflict of goals within an organisation. For example, while production wants low complexity, large manufacturing batches and high utilisation, good customer service requires a high degree of flexibility or frequent and often smaller manufacturing quantities. The second example is probably not tangible or influenceable enough for many corporate functions to identify with it and derive correct measures. In fact, customer service faces many challenges along a supply chain, including the procurement of components, demand planning, warehousing and distribution to customers.

Ultimately, I find a mixture and fair weighting of several perspectives (see the triangle: service, costs, capital) optimal. A high level of transparency regarding the chosen indicators within the management team, and among our team members, supports result delivery. This includes regular status updates with an assessment of the situation and likely corrective measures or consequences.

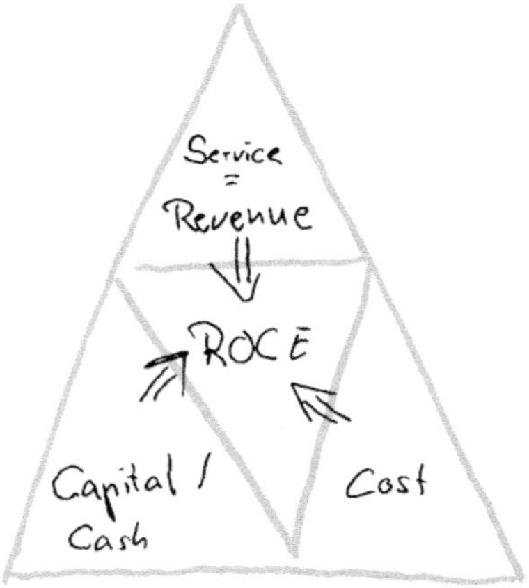

(1) Revenue − Costs = EBIT

(2) $\frac{\text{EBIT}}{\text{Capital}} = \text{ROCE}$

(based on Desired)

4 - Digging into the Planning Details

I still commute between Switzerland and the Czech Republic. I fly from Zurich to Prague on Mondays and back on Fridays. It's about time that we find permanent accommodation. Sophia hasn't been to the Czech Republic yet, but will finally visit me next week, as she has been invited for a job interview. She has made it clear that she will not move without local employment. I'm very concerned about this and have shared this with my employer over the last few weeks. They have promised to support us and help Sophia look for employment opportunities, internally and externally. Meanwhile, there are two options, one of which is the said interview. She will have to be downgraded to a local salary, but there are countless international companies in Prague that will also be good for her development and experience.

My compensation as an expatriate will nevertheless raise our joint disposable income well above what we are used to from our parents' homes. At the end of the day, we are currently independent, have no children or other obligations yet and should therefore put financial motives to the back of our minds. Anyway, I agreed to the relocation without any draft contract or agreement on a compensation package. Maybe I'm naïve or my view of the world is too positive, but so far, I've always done well: "Do a good job and show what you can achieve, then recognition usually follows automatically".

This afternoon I meet the relocation agents assigned to us. At the factory gate, two young ladies welcome me and drive with me into town. We look at two residential properties. As soon as my address is fixed, we want to do the residence registration together and exchange my driving licence for a local EU version. I'm glad to have such good guidance in these matters. Linguistically and also in terms of time, this is a great relief and another privilege of a professional secondment.

The flats are each unique in their own way. The first property consists of three floors and ends in a kind of tower on the top floor. However, the location is too central for me in the city, and I'd have to deal with too much traffic in the morning when I drive to the factory. It is also too far from the tram. Since Sophia won't be taking a car, I want her to have good public transport connections and be able to get anywhere in this big city within an hour's drive. I just really need her interview to go successfully, as they say, "Happy wife, happy life". My biggest worry is that I'll be absorbed in my work, and she'll suffer at home like a traditional housewife, far away from her family and friends.

The second flat is in Prague 6, in the Vokovice area. The local transport connections and the location not too far away from the city centre sound promising. Another positive point is that it's in the right direction, to the north. We drive to a fenced-off residential area and pass security. The real estate in the whole area seems impressive. The buildings are new and are a mixture of single-family houses and apartment buildings. The construction is very modern and features a mixture of various building materials such as wood, stone, concrete and glass. All windows are floor-to-ceiling, terraces or balconies are completely glazed. I enquire whether the budget allocated by the company is sufficient, as I feel at home even before entering the apartment. Fortunately, the question is answered positively. The flat is on the first floor and consists of three rooms and a kitchen-living room. I call Sophia to check with her directly and send her the details by e-mail. Ten minutes later, I ask the agents to initiate the rental of this flat. I hope we'll feel at home soon.

The two women finally drive me to my hotel and say goodbye. The next morning Marek will pick me up, as my company car is still at the factory.

The first meeting of the day is with my own team. For today, I've arranged several individual sessions with the operational buyers, i.e., the material planners. The main task of these colleagues consists of daily contact with the more than fifty packaging and raw material suppliers. These are very operational tasks such as order arrangements, information exchange on expected deliveries, complaints management or invoice control. I have already looked at some evaluations and see that our suppliers have a poor adherence to schedules and quantities. In the production reporting, I also discovered a regular lack of material during the execution of production orders. In addition, write-offs are made in the warehouse for expired raw materials or components that are no longer needed due to changes in the bill of materials. In the last few days, I have had to approve some invoices for demurrage from our transport providers who could not unload ordered materials and thus the trucks had to remain on our factory premises over the weekend. I am keen to understand if the team is aware of these problems and what their root cause assessment will look like.

Ondrej attends the meetings, and I notice that his colleagues are constantly looking at him as if to say, "Please let him answer the questions and take control of the discussion".

"Do we have data that show a trend in delivery performance, i.e., have individual suppliers become worse or better?", I start.

As expected, Ondrej takes the lead. "As you can see, our reports show that the performance of the most important suppliers, in terms of quantity but also on-time delivery, has stagnated over the last two years."

"Yes, I see that, but are we satisfied with the result? I have a higher expectation of our partners!"

"But we don't achieve better results because central procurement offers little support and is only interested in low procurement costs now."

"Ok, I understand, but first, please explain to me the parameters for calculating the delivery performance metric. I want to be sure we are cleaning our own house first before we focus on other functions."

"I don't understand," Ondrej replies.

"Well, please show me with which delivery times and quantity variances we calculate the ratio and what is agreed in the supplier contract."

"We have no contract data."

"Good, then let's obtain and analyse the contracts of the largest suppliers by purchase quantity. We'll talk more this afternoon. Please call the procurement department. The contracts should be centrally available there."

Ondrej looks at me in disbelief.

Five hours later, we continue our morning conversation. This time only the two of us sitting together, as Ondrej's team has already gone home for the day.

"So, what did you find out?"

"I received the contracts immediately. Here are the relevant documents."

We look at the first contract - it's for a supplier of cardboard packaging. The contract states that the order lead time is at least six weeks - on the condition that the supplier receives a rolling call-off forecast from us and that the purchase order may deviate from the forecast by a maximum of twenty-five per cent, at least in the first twelve weeks of the planning horizon. Furthermore, it is written in the conditions that deliveries can be over- or under-delivered by ten per cent.

"Could you please show me the master data in the system for this particular supplier and the associated materials?"

Ondrej opens the ERP system and shows various examples to me. He starts looking a little disappointed.

"It looks like we don't comply with the order lead times and haven't stored any quantity tolerances. But that shouldn't be a problem, so maybe it's just our supplier evaluation that's wrong."

"Are you sure about that? How do we know if our goods will arrive in time before the scheduled production date of our finished goods?"

"The supplier calls us in case of delays or changes in quantity and we make bilateral arrangements, so everything is fine."

"On the contrary, I think many of these arrangements are unnecessary and waste all parties involved a lot of time that could be invested better." I continue, "So, what happens if the supplier pushes the deadline so far back that production cannot take place as planned?"

"Then there is a change of plan, and we just produce the product a little later."

I refrain from commenting further because this is precisely where one of our challenges lies. How are we going to get stability into the production plans if we put ourselves in a situation where we constantly have to adjust the plans? What's most concerning to me is that Ondrej doesn't seem to think that this might be an issue for our customers. We may also incur unnecessary set-up costs in production because we have to change over our production lines and separate product groups.

After a pause for thought, I ask, "And what about the call-off forecast?"

"What exactly do you mean by that?"

"In simple terms, an image of the medium-term production plan broken down to component level with the help of the bill of materials of the finished products. It also takes into account the associated material loss rates and order lead times. Possibly also the order lead-time to offset production date and expected goods receipt."

"We don't have anything like that."

"Why not?"

"Because we rarely plan beyond the next eight weeks, so there's no reliable production schedule available after about the third month of the planning horizon."

"So how do we know if we or our suppliers are running into bottlenecks or potential item delivery shortfalls?"

"Excuse me, but we're talking about long-standing business relationships. I trust that our suppliers will contact us in time to make appropriate arrangements."

"How is the supplier supposed to know if or how our demand will change in the future? We have a lot of product changes or design adjustments. I suppose our sales forecasts need improvement as well?"

Silence ...

"Ondrej, take another look at the performance indicators we discussed earlier. We have many missing parts or on the other hand, wrong components in stock. Should we leave it like this and just continue to work as usual?"

He becomes embarrassed but doesn't respond.

I let some time pass, then make a suggestion. "In the next few days, please draft a process including the corresponding template for future communication with our suppliers. I'm not talking about regular orders here, but a non-binding call-off forecast. Let's say, for starters, over at least the next six months. And importantly, it should be a rolling process, meaning weekly, monthly or quarterly recurring depending on the segmentation of our suppliers."

"You do understand that we don't have reliable production schedules for the mentioned period?" I notice his snide undertone.

"Let me worry about that. I'll be sitting down with Leos the day after tomorrow to discuss this very topic." I stop myself from giving him a sideways glance to see whether he has already thought of talking to the responsible production planners about this very topic.

Two weeks have passed since my one-on-one meeting with Leos. Today he's supposed to demonstrate what he meant by his statement regarding output or volume fluctuations in production. After some small talk, he projects a large amount of data on the screen.

I surprised – in a positive way – because he really put a lot of effort into it. The presentation could be a bit more professional, but that is not important here and now. We'll work on that together before we present his findings to the factory management

"Gabriel, I have analysed the production plans for the last three months."

"Well, go on." I have to stop myself, as I'm often impatient and would like to ask a few questions immediately.

"The starting point is the plan that I've agreed with Pavel's department, which we align and approve every Thursday for the following week before we release the production orders to the shop floor."

"Just to clarify, why don't we take a plan that we have made, for example, three weeks in advance - wouldn't that be more appropriate as we cover the pre-aligned campaigns of product groups and some of the order lead times for pre-products and components in a better way?"

"I understand your point, but please wait for my conclusion because you'll see that our process doesn't seem mature enough for that."

"Agreed."

"Against Thursday's plan, I compared the actual production output for the week. With a few exceptions, many production orders show differences, some of them considerable."

"Could you give me some examples, please."

"Well, the week before last, we had twenty production orders on our large glass filling line with over five hundred tonnes of planned output. But in fact, only twelve orders were produced of the planned quantity. Here I even allowed a tolerance of plus or minus ten per cent deviation. The total quantity produced by the production line fell short by about twenty per cent.

"Were some items produced that were not planned for or other products significantly overproduced?"

"Yes, that was the case. There seems to be a trend. The larger the planned batch size of an order, the more likely it is to be overproduced. Smaller or tail stock-keeping units are not produced at all or are significantly underproduced."

"I notice in your table that there are large production orders, especially towards the end of the production week. Why is that?"

"Well, Pavel wants to be able to continue producing with good line performance, i.e., allow for overachievement. It should be ensured that packaging material or semi-finished products are available for this."

My next question is particularly important to me. "Do we adhere to the agreed capacities? By this, I mean are we planning orders within the production hours which are in line with the agreed shift pattern or are we sometimes placing production orders outside the available time?"

Leos goes red in the face and points out that Vladimir and Pavel have given him a clear instruction: No matter what, he has to place orders as a placeholder at the end of the week.

"Please help me, Leos, I can't keep up here. You show me a report of the fulfilment of the production plan. This evaluation seems to be proof that we have less inventory in the finished goods warehouse at the end of each production week compared to our original plan. In addition, we are forced to place additional orders into the plan. And we know that based on demonstrated performance we may not realise that output. Isn't that a double negative effect?"

"But surely our ultimate goal is to achieve high production efficiency."

"Says who?", I interject energetically.

"Well, everyone. Starting with the plant manager and especially everyone in production."

"I think we're shooting ourselves in the foot. In my world, stable but especially consistent planning is the starting point for a smoothly functioning supply chain. And above all, it's indispensable to have a reliable projection of, for example, realistic inventory ranges, production quantities and product availability issues. Of course, there will always be changes to a plan, but that doesn't matter for now. As soon as we have more operational freedom in the process, the learning curve can set in and there will be fewer negative influences on production and thus ultimately efficiency increases."

"But you know Vladimir. He hardly gives me any room to make my own decisions. What am I supposed to do now?"

"Good point, but I'm in charge of the planning function now, and there is a reason why I'm here. Because, together, we need to optimise the site's supply chain performance and particularly increase customer service results. To do that, we'll make changes that not everyone will like in the first place. But we're going to try to bring everyone along on our journey."

"What are we doing now, specifically?"

"I suggest two things. Firstly, please create an evaluation at item level in which you show the routing master data as this is the base with which your production plan is created. You should compare this with the actual historical data, i.e., the demonstrated output. Something like "quantity per hour target" vs. "quantity per hour actual". With that information, we'll visit production together next week, walk the lines with Pavel and check our understanding."

"Understood, I can do that. And what is your second suggestion?" Leos now seems confident, and I imagine that he likes our approach, which is to use figures, data and facts.

"Well, that will be another assignment for you. I would like you to work out a proposal with the team mates on how we can ensure that we have enough reserves of material and can accommodate production in case of overproduction opportunities. Please also consider whether this approach makes sense for all lines."

Actually, I want to talk about the planning horizon. I want to figure out the reasons why we sometimes plan only eight weeks into the future and how we can arrive at twelve to eighteen months of rolling production planning soon. But what I've just learned shows that we have such a poor foundation that any medium- or long-term planning will only be on shaky ground. I won't forget about that ambition, but I won't tackle it for a few weeks until I agree with Leos's findings and suggestions.

I go back to my desk, satisfied. Someone calls my name from behind me. I recognise from the voice that it is Vladimir. He engages me in a friendly conversation, inquires whether we have already found a house and when we're moving. He seems genuinely interested in how I'm settling in so far. Then the mood shifts a bit. He asks me to come to his office so we can talk privately without being disturbed. Once seated there, he gets straight to the point.

"You came with such high praise, but so far you haven't made any impact. Our numbers are bad, as usual, and I also have the impression that you're giving the team strange ideas. Ondrej is super frustrated because you don't seem to recognise his work and experience and Leos, who really doesn't know much about planning, is eager to support your analyses and investigations instead of doing the things I ask him to do."

"Thank you for your openness". I say this just so I can take a breath. Otherwise, I tend to counterattack and then it turns into a nasty discussion without added value and increased frustration is guaranteed.

"I'm now in my second month at the site. Most of the team seems to be gaining trust in me and many are starting to understand my philosophy."

"That's nice to hear, but what specifically are you doing right now? We don't need more evaluations and above all you should concentrate on the sales organisations and not cause trouble internally among the departments."

"What trouble are you talking about?"

"Well, Pavel has complained to me that he is under the impression that you are questioning his KPIs and are now starting to control production."

"With our good line efficiencies, we shouldn't have anything to hide," I counter. In retrospect, that was a bit unwise, as I deliberately provoke him.

Vladimir jumps right on it, "Have you ever headed production? I don't think so."

"Stop, let's not keep talking in this tone, please. Trust me. I'm not here to satisfy my ego but because I want to help the factory deliver better results in a sustainable way. I'm no longer a stranger from headquarters but part of the leadership team. Give me some time and you'll see in which direction we're going. I'm sure we have some inconsistencies in our internal processes that we need to correct as soon as possible." I know Vladimir is under tremendous pressure. He has had to hand over responsibility to me and knows that the decision-makers at headquarters, people like Pieter, do not support him.

"But I want you to concentrate on our customers. You know very well that the demand planning, or rather the forecasting quality of the future sales plans, leaves a lot of room for improvements. That's our main problem, not whether we make a bit more or less volume each week."

"I only partially agree with this. Yes, the forecasting quality needs to be improved - we'll work on that soon enough. But my working hypothesis today is that the fluctuations generated by us to our suppliers and in our production create just as much disturbance in the supply chain as inaccurate sales planning. The supply side fluctuations are much easier to control, as these are primarily caused by us, rather than influencing any customers, sales teams or marketing folks."

"Well, you know how to talk the talk! Let's hope results follow. Nevertheless, please give greater priority to my point."

We end the conversation and I think we can both be satisfied with the outcome. Still, it's a little hard for me not to be upset.

5 - A Surprise Visitor

Today we're leaving Switzerland. Sophia and I sit in a café in the centre of Schaffhausen and have breakfast. Meanwhile, at home, the removal company is packing our things and dismantling the first pieces of furniture. You can't move any more relaxed than that, we think to ourselves. The cleaning of the flat for the handover and the approximately six-hour drive by car to our new hometown will be the most exhausting part. We didn't need to organise customs clearance or hard-working helpers. We are grateful to my employer for this benefit because it allows us to be more relaxed about the exciting journey and upcoming challenges ahead.

Besides the excitement, however, we both feel a little melancholy. Sophia's family lived a few minutes' drive away. In the future we will see them less often. I'm used to moving regularly, but it seems every time I finally settle down, I have to break away again and leave a lot behind. The older I get, the more difficult it becomes to make intimate connections, as you often end up in very established circles of friends or sports clubs. I imagine, at least at the moment, that this is the price of a successful career. Sophia's parents and siblings have also become a kind of family for me. In addition, I have met new friends through my recently completed further education in business administration who have similar motivations in life. We discussed our further paths together - did we want to get a master's degree in Austria, or should we get into adult education and give lectures ourselves for specialists or business economists? In the sports club, I recently succeeded in establishing personal connections with some individual club members. This was rather difficult due to my many business trips.

Before I let myself fall deeper into melancholy, I think about the opportunities this constant change provides: the people and personalities I've been able to meet and get to know or experience and the wisdom I've collected. This has only been possible because I keep embracing change and taking risks.

Two days later we are sitting in our new flat, both enjoying a glass of red wine. The boxes are all unpacked and you would think we've been living here for a while. I'm happy we are walking this path together. Sophia supports me a lot, but she is also much less restless compared to me. I look across the table in love and compliment her. For her, too, a new stage of life begins tomorrow. She passed the job interview a few weeks ago with flying colours and will start a new job in the centre of Prague. I sincerely hope she'll enjoy her work and be well received by her new colleagues.

As if the last few days have not been exciting enough, a surprise awaits me the next morning. Our management team is sitting down for a routine meeting. Suddenly the mood changes because Alex, our plant manager, explains that he will be changing jobs internally. He doesn't provide any further details for now but refers to a new interim factory manager. He should be arriving any moment. Marek has just picked him up from the airport. We take a break and get a coffee. The wildest speculations begin, but we are also disappointed that Alex is leaving. He has been able to develop the team during the last difficult months and created a positive mindset and team spirit. Sure, some performance indicators are not yet at desired levels, but we think we're on the right track.

I look out of the window onto the factory premises. Marek passes security and parks his blue car in front of the office building. The moment his passenger leaves the vehicle, I get a flashback. The man with the long coat, black leather bag and grey hair first goes into the smoking area and lights a cigar – it's Pieter Smith. I feel a big grin come over my face. It makes me a little uncomfortable, as I'm sure I'm the only one of the managers who will be happy to welcome this guest. I also feel bad for Alex, not knowing whether he is switching internally voluntarily or whether it was strongly suggested to him.

I run down the stairs and go to Pieter.

From a distance, I call out, "Hi Pieter. Good to see you."

Using a Dutch expression, he calls back, "*Jongen*, how are you?" while the corners of his mouth tighten into a grin. "I guess you'll have to deal with me for a while. How's the team's mood?"

We talk briefly about rather trivial things and then walk towards the meeting room together. I notice how some of my colleagues react in shock to his arrival. Vladimir, in particular, looks at us in surrender. He had a heated argument with Pieter during a conference call a few weeks ago.

The meeting that follows Pieter's arrival will resonate with me for a long time. We sit around the meeting table like schoolchildren being scolded because Pieter formulates very clearly and precisely what he expects from us and what needs to be stopped or improved immediately. The crisis manager with his "command and control" breaks out of him. He shares that the company is currently looking for a new plant manager and that he is planning to stay at our plant for about six months. His declared goal is to put needed basics and needed groundwork in place before a new factory head arrives.

He singles me out from my colleagues. I even have the feeling that he is giving me a particularly hard time. He asks me provocatively and in front of the whole team, "Gabriel, are you in charge of a planning or a re-planning department? We didn't send you to the Czech Republic so you could take a company-paid holiday."

I don't take it personally and imagine he just wants to motivate me. His statement makes me understand that I should speed up and deliver results sooner rather than later. Nevertheless, I want to initiate the upcoming changes based on my own philosophy. It will be an interesting balancing act.

At some point, I stop counting the *godverdommes* (goddamnits) that Pieter throws at us as he lists all our performance issues and failures. One would think that we have nothing under control. We're back to the point where my professional optimism kicks in and I think that sometimes you have to tear things down in order to build them back better.

6 - Tour of the Production Halls

The dust has settled, and normality has returned to our everyday factory life. I'm still trying to improve certain basics of our planning processes.

Before Leos and I visit the shop floor, we go through his analysis at my desk. He jumps straight into the subject. "I'll explain briefly what I've done, then I'll show you the result."

"Well, go ahead – I'm curious."

"I've captured the output of each individual product per production line. In the first columns of the table, you see the target data, i.e., the agreed planned quantity per hour maintained in the routing master data. The following columns show the actual data, in our case the actual quantity produced per item and the time spent on it."

"I understand. What time horizon did you apply to draw the data?"

"I've used the last twelve months but have checked whether a different period would significantly change the outcome. There seems to be no noticeable difference."

This little detail pleases me because he demonstrates a good ability to work with the data.

He continues, "Now I've converted the actuals into quantities per hour, compared them with the planned quantities and weighted the delta of the production quantity. Here you see the result". He points to a Gantt chart.

Before looking at the result, I praise Leos for his logical approach and especially the two details - the validation of the considered period as well as the weighting of the individual results so that smaller production orders in terms of quantity do not have an overvalued influence on the overall result. I once read in the book *The 5-Minute Manager* that praise is better received if you articulate "why" you are praising somebody, i.e., what was particularly good.

Now my eyes rest on the diagram. I see that not one of the production lines is even close to the target output. In the best case, the actual quantity deviates by ten per cent, in the worst case I recognise twenty-five per cent. This delta seems very high to me, and so I ask a question to clarify, "What exactly does the deviation reveal? I'm aware that we produce about ten thousand pallets per week of finished goods. A negative deviation of twenty-five per cent, i.e., a quarter, would mean that we do not produce, stock or ship two thousand five hundred pallets to customers, although we project this in our plans".

"Yes, that's right," Leos replies without hesitation, adding, "I was also surprised at how much of a difference it makes".

We leave for the shop floor and meet with Pavel as agreed. Leos and I want to validate the data on the spot before we forward it to other departments at the plant. We put on our safety shoes, vest and hairnet then start walking.

A little later, Pavel leads us through the production halls. Strictly speaking, we're talking about three buildings. The first one is dedicated to the production of salad dressings and ketchup as well as mayonnaise. A new filling line for jars has just been transferred to us after a plant closure in the Netherlands and is in the "ramp-up" phase and will mainly produce mayonnaise for England. This will significantly increase the production volume of our factory. The remaining filling and packaging lines are somewhat smaller in size but have a rather complex portfolio of recipes and packaging formats associated with them.

The second hall hosts the production of margarine - cubes for baking or frying, tubs of spreadable vegetable fats or even dairy cream alternatives are produced and packaged here. Without Pavel, I would have got lost long ago. In the buildings everything is nested and has grown over many decades, which can be seen in the mixture of old and new installations and equipment. Cables run everywhere, countless pipes and many electronical cabinets are installed. I stop in front of some of the machines and admire the precision with which thousands of carton boxes are folded and glued per hour or how even more tubs are filled with margarine. I'm always as excited as a little child when I'm on the shop floor. It makes the administrative work tangible and brings all the numbers on our computer screen to life.

We will not even look at the third production area today, as it is excluded from the analysis. Unfortunately, the vitamin shots have been a flop so far and the sales organisations are not selling anywhere near the quantities we need to amortise the millions of euros invested.

During the tour, we show the prepared data to Pavel and check several parameters. We want to understand which machine parts determine the target performance for the individual products to be manufactured. Is it the bottleneck machine? This means the slowest unit along the chain of line modules. This could be the case packer, for example, which can pack fewer pieces per hour of margarine tubs than the tubs filler specifies. Fortunately, Pavel confirms that in his understanding the main line module, in our case the filler, i.e., the most expensive single module, determines the output.

We also differentiate output data depending on size of primary packaging material or recipe complexity. The figures match those of Leos. For example, the machine supplier specifies the filler nameplate speed of three hundred and sixty tubs per minute, but certain recipes can only be run with less product to the filler, and thus, we reduce the machine output to, say, three hundred tubs per minute. Another example may be that a two-hundred-and-fifty-gram tub runs much slower speed compared to a double-sized tub with five hundred grams of margarine. We also agree on the following: If a downstream module can process less output, the nominal speed of the production line remains unchanged, but the utilisation rate or efficiency of the affected products is reduced to calculate the expected pieces per hour. And it is precisely this data that my team would have to mirror in the master data and apply to the official production planning.

We go through various examples of individual production lines. I can't help myself and interject, "What are these data aligned with if they are obviously wrong?"

Pavel shrugs his shoulders. "Well, we, that is, your department and I, share proposals during the annual budget planning cycle. Our figures are regularly adjusted by Operational Accounting afterwards. In the end, their guidelines end up in the system."

"Ok, that smells pretty much like corporate politics interfering here. I assume that our plant controller Martin has to adhere to various requests and wishes from headquarters."

Leos looks at me in astonishment and asks, "What are the reasons for manipulating target figures?"

"Well, this data is ultimately not only used for our operational supply chain planning but is also the basis for the price calculation of our finished products. If we store better efficiencies or overstated nominal line speeds in the master data, lower manufacturing costs are reflected in the price or cost of goods calculation."

Now Pavel also gets it. "Ha, well that's why I'll probably experience constant standard costs deviations. I've been really torn apart in performance meetings over the last few months because we don't have our costs under control."

Good point, I think.

"But we still have a problem. If we adjust the planning data to the actual output, then our costs don't really disappear. We just report them correctly in the first place. At least this way our sales companies would work with the correct costs of goods sold, which in turn would allow them to calculate profit margins correctly and possibly reconsider the selling prices of our products."

"I know, Gabriel, we need to increase efficiencies. That way we can make more volume per hour and eventually reduce operational shifts, i.e., working time, or relocate volumes back into our factory that we are currently outsourcing."

"That's right," I reply and add, "But we should take it one step at a time. I'll talk to Martin about what we can do to map the right operational data in the system as quickly as possible. We'll discuss the topic of increasing efficiency another time. Here we should talk about batch sizes, article groupings and the complexity of our product portfolio. We also have to involve Marketing and Sales. One question could be: should we keep individual products in the assortment, or can certain articles achieve a higher degree of harmonisation in their packaging or formulation?"

Leos and I go back to our open-plan office. We are satisfied and continue discussing our findings for a while. I ask him to use the new data sets, i.e., the demonstrated output, to calculate a capacity requirement for the coming months per production line and show it to me in the form of a Rough-Cut Capacity Plan.

"We agreed on one more point for today," I say as soon as Leos has written down his notes.

"Exactly, we wanted to talk about overproduction."

"Correct. We have learnt today that our production performance needs to improve. Therefore, we should support Pavel and his team to produce more as soon as they have the chance for more quantity." I add, "Have you thought about what this overstating of the production volumes means?"

"I'm a little confused. We over-estimate the production volume twice in the worst case, at least that became more than clear to me after our conversation today. In bad production weeks we don't even get the planned quantity within the available working time. Then if I add a production order or two at the end of the weekly cycle, that extra quantity doesn't come either."

I encourage him to continue speaking as his thoughts and formulations are on the right track.

"Over-planning then leads to less quantity available in our finished goods warehouse for dispatch to the sales companies. This means that I permanently fail to meet my stock targets, and this can even trigger delivery shortfalls, i.e., backorders or out of stocks that we didn't project in our plans."

I nod contentedly and add, "And it is precisely these unforeseen delivery shortfalls that lead to us constantly sitting in escalation meetings instead of fixing the underlying problems. In addition, we are repeatedly making false promises to our partners along the supply chain."

"I'm already pretty excited about the capacity evaluations. If I can make less volume per hour, then I need more time, i.e., capacity, to make the total demand. We have often had to add unplanned extra shifts over the weekends. Many operators in production are frustrated by this."

"Yes, I've already seen the result of the latest staff survey. And will you continue to add additional production orders over the available capacity?"

"Well, when we have revised the master data, the problem we just discussed will become smaller. I think we could leave it like that."

I'm not angry with him, he's just still too inexperienced and so I ask more questions.

"Last week we achieved a good output on the new glass line we received from the Netherlands. So, the planned quantity and actual quantity within the working time was fulfilled well. Nevertheless, I observe in the production plan a large additional order on Saturday. There was no working time agreed for that day. What happened as a result?"

"Yes, that's right. Because we are in the ramp-up of the line, we have to make sure that we can produce more at any time. The demand from England is high and our stocks are very low. I think it's no problem that the order has not been fulfilled."

I have to correct him. "Well, we were just talking about the fact that this over-planning leads to false inventory projections. This means that this one order generates calculated stock that in reality will never be in our warehouse. But our planning logic and the planning software continue to calculate with that extra quantity. As a result, we underestimate the future production requirements, production plans have to be changed at short notice and the material requirements at our suppliers for raw and packaging materials also change."

He agrees with me and says, "Ah, now I understand another dilemma. This morning I spoke to Magdalena, and she mentioned the recurring problems with piling up deliveries in the packaging warehouse. On Friday and Saturday there were various inbound trucks with empty jars that we couldn't unload. She told me about the invoices for demurrage. The warehouse was once again fully utilised and due to the additional quantities of our new production line, we have to plan according to demand, like almost just-in-time, in order to cope with the scarce storage space. The annoying thing is that the requirements for the empty glasses were triggered by my additional production order, which was intended as a placeholder only."

I'm impressed that Leos learns so quickly. He seems to understand well the end-to-end interdependencies of planning with all factory areas, and I'm convinced that he has what it takes to be a good supply planner.

"Well spotted, Leos! And that's exactly why we have to evaluate for which products and which quantities we can and want to keep an additional safety stock of materials on-site. We can coordinate this together with the warehouse and production teams and establish a process for how these additional quantities can be realised – without overstating production plans."

He leaves my desk and says, "Great, thanks for your support – I already have an idea!"

7 - Optimising Tactical Planning

I'm working long hours. Sophia often only gets to see me for dinner, after which I grab the laptop and answer some e-mails or create presentations. This is a consequence of my working style, as I prefer to plan my days on-site with personal meetings and conversations instead of working on e-mails alone at my desk. I find the personal exchange much more value-adding, especially with such a young team that wants to be inspired and still needs to gain lots of experience. The work that I do autonomously, I can do from anywhere.

I spend a lot of time with individual team members, especially with Jana and the other team leaders. For this purpose, we meet in the informal meeting areas of the management building – for one thing, we can discuss things more confidentially here away from the open-plan office, and for another, I enjoy the change of scenery as I don't like to spend too much time at my desk. Pieter likes to make fun of me and asks if I'm flirting again or working – a reference to the high percentage of women working in the Planning department.

There is one principle that I've adhered to since I've been in a relationship with Sophia: not to work at weekends. That time belongs to us. Especially since I'm heavily involved at work, I'm not a good partner to Sophia during the week. I must not forget that she moved countries and gave up all her social contacts to support my personal development. Therefore, for her sake, I also have to invest time in us as a couple – this compensation is of course also good for me, and with the Czech capital we have plenty of leisure time possibilities and places to discover. We try to eat out twice a week in one of the city's wonderful restaurants. Sometimes in more touristy corners, other times very local. It's like two worlds we walk between. The simple and very traditional Czech life, but also the glittering, elitist big city feeling. There is also a lot going on culturally in the city and we went to the ballet just the other day. Next week we've booked tickets for the performance of *Carmen* at the State Opera. Sophia enjoys these events. I've grown to like them too, but I prefer going to the cinema, even if the movie is in English. It seems Sophia is getting along well and that her homesickness is waning over time. I hope that's the case.

The current working week is themed "optimising tactical planning". According to my understanding, the period of interest spans the fourth to the eighteenth month of the rolling planning horizon. I also want to tackle the "improvement of demand planning" promised to Vladimir, or at least try to understand where and how we can start on that topic.

Both topics need to be prepared for an upcoming event. Pieter, Vladimir and I have agreed that we will invite all our internal customers, i.e., the supply chain managers and key planners of the receiving countries of our goods, to our factory. The content of the event will be a workshop for better aligned planning between the sales organisations and our factory, highlighting already identified improvement measures, a little PR for our plant and, last but not least, a kind of team building. We want to take advantage of the charms of Prague and go out for dinner and later dive into the nightlife. It's important to Pieter that we don't forget to have fun in addition to the hard work and challenges we face. From experience, I can confirm that you often get along better even with co-workers who are difficult to deal with in a relaxed atmosphere and can also overcome solid arguments with a good conversation and, above all, laughter and fun. In this way, the private side becomes visible beneath the professional businessperson.

Jana and Magdalena are sitting opposite me. We are in the middle of the topic of demand planning and are verifying if we have a common understanding. First, we record the flow of goods from the factory to the warehouse and final point of sale. We check whether our system configuration also maps these flows correctly. Since we are talking about demand planning, i.e., sales forecasting, we have to identify the final point of sale within our intra-company supply chain. In our case, the customer sales take place in the country of the sales organisations in the form of a distribution centre, i.e., customer-facing warehouse. This is where the goods leave our company, and we invoice the external customers upon pick-up or delivery. Fortunately, these transfer points are properly mapped in our planning system. Therefore, we assume that our sales forecast shall be planned against these locations. Via backward planning, the distribution demand will be visible in our factory warehouse. Of course, doing so, the demand is converted into a net requirement for production planning utilising data like actual inventories, defined safety stocks or already planned inbounds. Aggregating these requirements incorrectly or not having the correct network footprint reflected in your planning system results in a very poor input for capacity, production or material planning. I'm glad we don't have to address this issue, as it would entail a major project involving IT and consulting services. Furthermore, we already receive the demand plans broken down into weekly buckets. This is also aligned with our weekly planning cycle, which we apply in production planning. I sigh with relief. "Well, then we have good preconditions and shouldn't allow excuses which may hinder improvements."

Now we go into several details to validate various of our working hypotheses.

"Jana, please show us an item that had particularly poor delivery performance in recent months, i.e., experienced quite a few non-deliveries or out of stocks."

"Here's a good example, the five-hundred-gram jars of mayonnaise in the Czech distribution centre."

"Good, now please compare the theoretical lost sales volumes to the difference between the forecast and the actual sales." We don't need to study the data for very long. It's immediately obvious that in the weeks with high non-deliveries, there was a significant portion of *lost sales* – in other words, we sell much less than forecast. I follow up, "Can you tell if the demand planners are projecting this trend into the future or are they manually adjusting the actual sales using the sales losses and original forecast as input?"

Magdalena looks at me and frowns. "Why is that important?"

"That's a good question. According to my knowledge, a sales forecast must reflect what is known as *unconstrained demand*. The word *unconstrained* is particularly important. By this I mean that the forecast should reflect the full sales potential across all sales channels or customers and not be artificially reduced by past supply shortages. An exception may be that we decide to keep demand low on purpose because, for example, expanding capacity at our plant is less lucrative from a business case perspective compared to the eventual additional sales revenue."

We look at other examples and we realise there is a recurring pattern of wrong forecasting. Thus, this may be a relevant topic for the planned workshop.

Inspired by these findings, we look for further indications of challenges in demand planning. Jana suggests taking a look at the most important products on the new glass line for England. She remembers that the British colleagues doubted our ramp-up curve during the commissioning period of the new production line and were already triggering unpleasant discussions at head office because they were expecting major delivery performance issues.

I like her idea.

Jana opens some files on her screen.

"Here you see the sales volumes of the last three years. Now I'll show you the sales forecast for the next twelve months."

We see strong volume growth especially in the next half year.

"Can this increase also originate from newly acquired customers or additional distribution in the retail sales channel?" Magdalena's question is relevant, and I ask her to look for the minutes of the latest escalation meetings with our English colleagues.

"Do the minutes contain anything about the underlying assumptions of their forecast?"

"It was noted that the market is stable or rather declining. There are also no additional promotions or other marketing activities planned to push sales. It was agreed within the relocation project team not to increase demand during the line's first year of operation at our site." I'm happy as this answers our question.

"What do you think would be the result of, let's say, inflating the demand plan?"

They both start talking almost simultaneously and come to the same conclusion: the forecasts contain buffer quantities to force us to plan for higher production output to ensure increased inventories and less likely delivery performance issues. It was actually agreed that we would build up an additional safety or project stock to buffer for eventually poor production output during ramp-up. And here lies a critical point. We have doubled the production requirement: on the one hand, the additional quantities in the sales forecast and on the other hand, the additionally built inventory. We'll also use these examples at our event to highlight current misconceptions in demand planning.

Before we conclude the meeting, we review the known performance indicators of a sales plan. This time we focus particularly on *forecast bias*, i.e., the difference between actual sales and originally forecasted volumes to show us the tendency of a too high or low demand plan. Calculated on the portfolio of products made at all our production lines, we see a bias of about fifteen per cent. If I convert this to our roughly ten thousand pallets of output per week, that adds up to one thousand five hundred pallets of which we sell either too much or too little compared to what is reflected in the original sales organisation's weekly forecast. This finding confirms my hypothesis that our internal fluctuations on the "supply side" - with two thousand five hundred pallets shortfall in production output per week - are greater than the volatility in sales planning generated by our customers.

In the afternoon, I go for a walk around the factory and see Pieter smoking a cigar whilst on a call. I join him once he's finished the phone call. We talk about the progress of the last few days, and I give him a summary of the past meeting, which focussed on demand planning. Pieter promptly replies, "Well, forecasts are usually wrong - a plan is nothing, planning is everything."

I nod and tell him that we want to tackle this topic during our workshop - but mention that I'm unsure how to explain this in a tangible but simple way. He thinks for a moment and takes a last puff from his cigar. "Let's go for a drink after work in the next few days, there's a bar right next to my hotel. We can play darts there too."

He walks back to his office, leaving me astonished.

8 - Rough Cut Capacity Plans

Sophia and I go to the opera and see the performance of *Carmen*. After the show, we stroll around Prague. At night the historic buildings are artfully illuminated, and you're immersed in another world. Here, too, I'm fascinated by the many bridges; there are said to be an estimated one hundred and eighty of these often historically relevant structures in the entire city area. From a hill we look towards the panorama of bridges, lit up by hundreds of lanterns. After our tour, we wait for the tram to Vokovice. We have a great view of Prague's Hradčany castle from the station. I still can't get enough of this city with its sights and impressions - whether day or night, I feel very comfortable living here, enjoying the time with Sophia.

As it got late last night, I stay in bed longer than usual. I forget that I've arranged a rather early - by my standards - meeting with Leos and Magdalena. I'm late, of course, but to apologise I bring croissants from the bakery I pass on my forty-five-minute commute.

We look at the topic of Rough-Cut Capacity Planning, i.e., our manufacturing capacity projections and utilisation. Magdalena attends the meeting because she usually coordinates the shift plans with the production management. She is well acquainted with valuable rules such as working time models or interdependencies amongst the production lines, for example shared upstream or downstream processes.

Leos uses a capacity model that was only recently introduced to him by Mike. In my previous role I supported Mike in the creation of that tool. We pursued the goal of creating a model that utilises similar data as used for operational production planning. At best, the needed parameters originate from ERP or the manufacturing execution system landscape. We wanted to ensure a common template which enables a similar look and feel when reviewing various production lines or machines. It should also be easy to use for regular updates. Leos introduces the model to Magdalena, referring to examples and actual data that he used for creating the capacity plan. He perfectly emphasises the need for aligned data. For example, the production efficiency must match the time available for planning production. He explains, "Since I've already deducted the start-up and shut-down times of the production line from the available time, I cannot use the OEE, *Overall Equipment Efficiency.* Otherwise, I would calculate various downtimes twice resulting in an understated available capacity. I have to rather make use of the individual item or format/recipe groups demonstrated production efficiency."

Entering a little hastily into the discussion, I ask, "How did you account for set-up and cleaning times during line changeover?"

"I've subtracted the changeover time from the available time, so we can manipulate it as another variable for simulation and figure out the impact on capacity utilisation when changing efficiency or set-up time." He adds that he recently met with Pavel to understand actual line performance. This ensures proper alignment before presenting and interpretating the capacity planning results.

I signal him a thumbs-up. Magdalena also seems impressed, as under Vladimir's influence she has not seen Leos so proactive and knowledgeable before. After further discussion, we stare at his modelling results. There is a diagram for each filling line that illustrates the respective capacity requirements for the coming months and compares them with the possible working time patterns. Some machines show a high utilisation rate, as suspected. For other lines, we even recognise demand peaks that exceed the agreed or possible shift models.

"Are the results a surprise to you?"

Magdalena confirms that by her intuition she already suspected that the coming months would be difficult to manage. She justifies it mainly on the basis of the additional volumes that our factory has received as a result of other sites being restructured.

I have to dig a little deeper. "Haven't you already been able to derive these insights from operational planning?"

"Look, Gabriel, we are only planning a few weeks into the future today. Roughly speaking, we have only created a feasible production plan for the next six to eight weeks, i.e., a plan that is matched to existing capacities or material availability. Any production orders beyond that eight-week period are not levelled. This triggers an overplanning of capacity in some weeks, but in turn we may not utilise the available capacity in weeks of low demand."

"But how do we then determine the required and optimal shift patterns for our production and warehouse staff?"

"We do this on the basis of historical data, for example the previous year. We have to stick strictly to the working hours agreed in the annual budget anyway."

"But looking at Leos's capacity plans, we need to change the agreed shift models. During high season we need more shifts, i.e., operating time. Out of season we could apply reduced working time models."

"Pavel says he wants to run a constant shift model all year round. He also believes in further increasing production efficiency and thus reducing the production time needed in the future."

"Ok, fair point, but that is still too simplistic for me. I don't see the improved production efficiencies nor favourable *total costs of ownership*. In our case, the levelling of production will force pre-production and thus build up much higher working capital in the form of finished goods inventories, which in turn may need to be stored at an overflow warehouse and trigger additional costs."

"Gabriel, you have to discuss this with Pavel. We've already lost several fights on that topic."

"I actually want us to run that Rough-Cut Capacity Planning exercise as a routine production planning task integrated into a monthly recurring planning process."

"We don't have the authority to regularly change shift patterns. Only the leadership team has the power to do so."

"Well, we will have to change that. You are much closer to the details and should be able to provide better recommendations for corrections and actions to the management team members who will participate in the monthly process. These decisions shall be taken based on the information you've prepared."

"You're seriously asking us to perform this time-consuming exercise each and every month?"

"Indeed, I am. I'm also convinced that you can automate parts of the process. Once the key parameters such as efficiencies, production time and specified output per hour are aligned with production and better understood by them, you will actually only have to import the latest demand. At best, in the future we will have optimised our planning system to the point where we can directly feed the monthly process with the system-generated planning data, which also covers the desired planning horizon of up to eighteen months."

They both look at me a little discouraged because of the expected extra workload.

"I can understand your scepticism. This is a new process to you. But I'm convinced that with improved alignment across all relevant value chain functions, we'll experience less firefighting. Plus, we don't have to re-plan the full eighteen-month horizon every week. Depending on the required lead time of our raw or packaging material suppliers and Pavel's restrictions regarding production flexibility, we could plan, say, only the first three months in a weekly rhythm. We would only need to reconcile demand and supply for the full long-term planning horizon once a month in the week of the monthly coordination meetings."

"What is the high-level objective of this process?"

"Good question. We need to reach a consensus plan across all stages of the supply chain. On the one hand, we need to be able to show our customers whether and how we can satisfy their demand plans. On the other hand, we have to make sure that our production plans are as accurate as possible, but also necessary, so that our suppliers can also align their supply chain plans with us."

"What do we do when we have capacity shortfalls?"

"That's precisely another motivation for this process. We have to check and decide how to deal with these issues. In some cases, our customers may have to postpone sales initiatives, or alternatively, we have to secure additional shifts and procure more components to meet peak demand. To do this, however, we have to take into account the relevant lead times for such decisions, for example the procurement of materials as well as adjusting production opening times."

"That sounds logical and reasonable, but what about the unreliable sales forecasts?" Leos now intervenes in the discussion.

"That's also a relevant point. We actually still have to identify how to tackle that topic. I would suggest that as long as there is no reduction in sales fluctuations, we have to keep a corresponding reactive capacity. That capacity shall enable short-term decisions on additional production orders but also ensure sufficient component availability. Alternatively, we simply need to hold higher finished goods inventory. That logic could also be a regular discussion point during our alignment meetings."

We end the meeting and my thoughts drift to Pieter's offer - an appointment for drinks and darts.

9 - Drinks and Darts

It's Wednesday evening. Pieter and I are sitting together in the bar near his hotel and we've both ordered a non-alcoholic beer. We start talking about the latest progress at our plant. In general, we are satisfied, because many indicators are trending in a positive direction. We still deliver a slightly worse delivery performance compared to some of our peer group factories, but we're gradually seeing a reduced number of customer complaints. We're spending much less time on escalation calls or other crisis meetings. Instead, we proactively communicate both good and bad news to our customers, including details of cause and effect. This does not go unnoticed by Pieter either, and he praises me, and the work of my team, for that improvement.

After a moment, he starts asking me about Vladimir, especially how we get along. I explain that on the surface we function well as a team, but our cooperation drains energy from both of us. This said, I quickly steer the discussion to our identified measures in production planning, telling him about the regular, rolling capacity planning to reconcile demand and supply. Even though Vladimir and I often have different opinions, I don't want to make disparaging comments about any colleagues behind their backs. Pieter goes along with the change of subject and listens attentively.

A little later, we talk about sales planning – perhaps the most important external input signal for steering our production site. Pieter confirms the need to address this topic more prominently. Above all, we should involve our colleagues at head office, such as Mike Pence, in the process. This way we don't have to deal with all the problems on our own. We can instead work out a standard template for demand planning improvements and support a pilot. Also, from a corporate politics point of view, we have to recognise that headquarters have more power to ensure awareness and prioritisation of needed forecasting improvements at our various sales organisations.

I tell him about the meeting I recently had with Jana and Magdalena and outline our hypotheses regarding inflated demand plans to force higher inventories or production output over real market demand. Also, the insufficient outlier cleaning of the market sales history, for example, out of stocks or special sales events, which will not repeat in the future, trigger a distorted demand signal, which is transferred into our production plans. We're on the same wavelength and discuss other common demand planning issues. We touch on the statistical analysis of historic sales, handling of backorders and promotional customer orders, along with leading indicators, such as labour market data and inflation.

Subsequently, we ask ourselves how well our commercial colleagues in Sales or Marketing are informed about competitor activities, such as promotions or product portfolio adjustments and their actual or expected supply issues. How is such information reflected in our short- or even medium-term forecasts? The weather and seasonality effect are also part of our discussion. After all, our portfolio contains several products that are strongly weather-dependent and thus have a pronounced seasonality. Good examples are the barbecues in summer, which give rise to a demand for salad dressings or the seasonal peak of margarine cubes for biscuit baking in December.

Pieter has the impression that our country supply chain managers are not well aligned with their commercial functions when it comes to demand planning. We agree that the message to the sales organisations must be that the country management team is responsible for a high-quality sales forecast. This team knows best which customers or tenders are being won or lost, which sales initiatives are planned or how the local portfolio is changing. Ultimately, the managing director must be able to sign-off the plan, with all its consequences in terms of costs and service and justify the underlying risks and opportunities. We must ensure that relevant changes in the sales forecast are communicated transparently and in alignment with the production sites or suppliers. At best, these market demand reviews shall be synchronised with the monthly rhythm we already proposed for capacity planning.

"It's good that we have similar thoughts, Pieter, but do you have any idea how we can make this topic tangible so we can pitch it at our upcoming workshop in an entertaining way?"

"That's one of the reasons we're here today. Let's throw some darts."

We play a few legs and order further drinks. By coincidence, I finish with three excellent shots: Two darts hit the outer bullseye and one goes in the inner bullseye. Pieter interrupts the game and asks me, "Do you know the difference between accuracy and precision?"

"No, aren't they synonyms?"

"Not exactly. Look carefully at your result. All three darts are placed close to each other. This is called precision."

"I see, and accuracy would be that I hit all the darts close to the optimum, for example the centre of the dartboard?"

"That's correct."

We continue playing and Pieter lands a bad performance. All the darts are spread across the board far away from the bullseye. "And what do you think?" he asks.

"I have no clue what you're getting at."

" I guess you're not as smart as you think sometimes". We laugh. "Those shots were inaccurate and imprecise."

The game continues, and when I hit all three darts in the sevens' segment, he asks again, "Now what?"

"Precise, but inaccurate!"

He nods and we continue. The final interruption of our game takes place during a round where the darts are quite central, but still scattered over different number segments. Confidently, I call out, "Accurate, but not precise!" Pieter seems impressed and pats me on the back.

"Thank you for this lesson, but what do I do now with the knowledge gained?"

"Well, now we need your imagination. Remember the four interrupted game plays and the positions of the darts." He hands me four napkins and a pen. "For each game situation, draw the darts as circles on these napkins, but without the dartboard.

"I don't understand what he's getting at but do as I'm told. We lay out the napkins with my drawings in front of us.

"What do you notice?"

"I don't know."

"Come on, try a little harder."

Some time passes before it dawns on me.

"If I focus solely on the circles and forget where they're placed, the precise results look very similar, even though one game was a success and the other a bad performance."

He signals me to keep talking.

"The imprecise results also tend to look similar."

"All right, but what's the bottom line?"

"If I don't know where or what the target is, then I can't judge whether the darts are placed accurately on the dartboard. I can only tell if they are precise, that is, close together."

"And that can be a message for our workshop with the countries. Future sales are our target and the country demand planners, with the help of their commercial functions, have the task of creating a plan that is as accurate as possible. They should spend less time adjusting the weekly or monthly fluctuations because high precision but poor accuracy does not help us at all. In the worst case, it actually wastes resources."

"You mean something like the saying: *it's better to be roughly right than precisely wrong*?"

I'm impressed how playfully he conveyed this lesson to me. We order a last drink and say goodbye a little later.

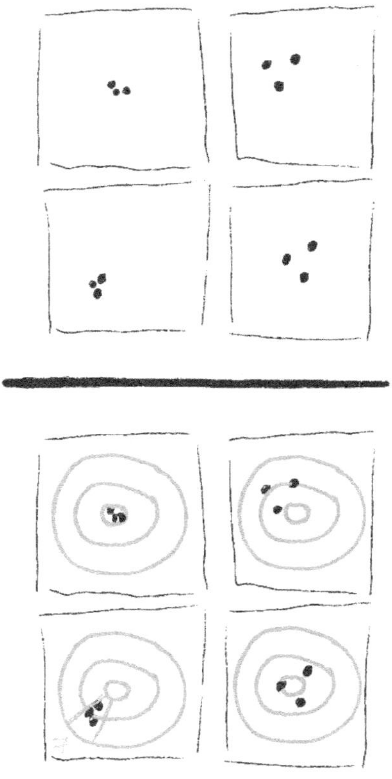

10 - Improving Material Supply

The next morning, I tell Sophia about the lightbulb moment. She can't follow and responds, amused, "If you present it like that at your workshop, you'll certainly ensure a clear message". Ok, my explanation could have been better and with a little more patience in explaining it, her sarcasm could have been avoided. I vow to try again at dinner, give her a hug and kiss her goodbye.

Fortunately, I only drank non-alcoholic beer yesterday, otherwise the coming discussion with Ondrej about the improvements in material planning would be even more difficult. My cynicism does not go unnoticed, and I have to caution myself to remain fair to Ondrej, even if our cooperation could be better at times. Somehow, we don't get along too well, and I increasingly have the impression that we're working against instead of with each other. I've noticed that he persistently meets with Vladimir. I tell myself that I'm perhaps overthinking this situation and should remain optimistic. After all, I keep talking about a culture of open doors and short decision-making processes. Thus, there should be nothing suspicious about my team spending time with other managers.

After walking through the office and wishing everyone good morning, I arrive at Ondrej's desk and ask if he's ready for our meeting.

"What did we want to look at again today?"

I hope he's joking, but we'll find out in a few minutes.

"We agreed that we would look at your suggestions for possible improvement measures regarding communication and alignment with our packaging and raw material suppliers."

"I still think that we shouldn't overdo it on our side and make it too convenient for our suppliers. We order, they deliver and, if necessary, get back to us if they foresee problems meeting our order deadlines or quantities."

I mumble something to myself and want him to sense my discomfort at this statement. "Our approach should rather be that we treat suppliers as a vital part of our extended supply chain and work in partnership."

"What do you mean by partnership?"

"This could be a form of an open exchange. For example, we enable each other more insight into planning data such as our future requirements and capacities. Or we hold joint workshops to understand how we can reduce lead times along the value chain and thus save costs, gain agility and improve service on both sides of business."

"I'm not sure if the suppliers have the right skills and capabilities to do so."

"That may be true, we also may not have them in our own organisation now. But somewhere we have to catch up, learn together and explore what is possible."

"I understand. Rome wasn't built in a day either. In the end, it will lead to increased workload for my team."

"That's also possible, but in the long run, I see these changes as an investment to have a stronger foundation in the near future. If we start building these skills today, we'll eventually be rewarded. We'll gain new insights and, most importantly, we'll spend less time firefighting material supply problems."

I believe that I've been able to outline my supply chain management approach and when we sit down together, I ask Ondrej to start with the actual topic and show what he has prepared.

"You mentioned a segmentation of the suppliers. In this table you see our suppliers sorted by order value. If we take this approach, we ll have to prioritise the suppliers with the highest procurement spend."

"Can you also create the list with number of orders and components purchased, that is, material numbers?"

Fortunately, the data is available and Ondrej has created a new pivot table in a few simple steps.

"This is the overview you want to see, but why?"

"Well, have a look directly at the first position on your table. If I see it correctly, this is a supplier of paper labels. We have hundreds of references that we order regularly. The value of the labels is very low, at least compared to empty glass jars or some special raw material."

"Yes, and that's why we usually order large quantities, as they hardly tie up any capital and take up little space in the warehouse. I see no reason to change anything here."

I ask him for patience and ask Jana if she can join us.

"Jana, we just talked the other day about possible reasons for last-minute changes in our production plans. Did we need to stop or re-plan any production orders recently because we were short of labels?"

She nods and describes three recent examples.

Ondrej intervenes energetically, "These are all anecdotes. The last case, for example, is related to a new product. Here, the graphic design, the artwork, was handed over too late to the supplier by Marketing."

"I'm disappointed that you're not engaging in this thought experiment, Ondrej. It's not about blaming anyone; it's about looking for potential for improvement. I can assure you that we are starting to build up reports that will show us on a weekly basis how often and why production orders are adjusted. This will be complemented by our new production fulfilment reporting. Then we will see how often, and above all, which materials run short or are missing."

"Understood, another report to look at and comment on."

"Don't be so negative," I say a little louder, causing several colleagues in the open-plan office to turn to us.

"But my point about new products and delays from the Marketing or Packaging Implementation team is certainly relevant as well."

"Yes, that's an important point. But I would also like to build up a broader responsibility for such product change or new product introduction projects in Planning in the future. Only we in Planning know when exactly a product must or can run on the production lines for the first time. In addition, we know our suppliers best, their lead times and dependencies such as manufacturing campaigns, prematerials and inventories or seasonal capacities. Therefore, I expect a material planner to keep an eye on project timing and any risks, and to get in touch with the production planner or Packaging Implementation to mitigate risks ahead of time."

I thank Jana, and after she leaves, we continue.

"So, what exactly are we doing now in terms of segmentation?"

"I suggest that we choose a mix of criteria, which we can correct later, on the basis of new findings. Why don't you and your team select the suppliers accordingly, one part with the highest procurement expenditure and the other part with the highest operational relevance? There will certainly be overlaps. How do we deal with such priority suppliers then?"

"Provided that our medium-term production plan becomes more reliable, we could actually start regularly sharing on some kind of material call-off forecast with key suppliers."

Ondrej shows me a transaction in our ERP system and introduces me to the formats in which the data could be extracted. Then we try to export to a file that could be processed by the data recipient accordingly, and he adds, "The differentiation between non-binding planned requirements and fixed purchase orders is problematic, but we could remedy this with a little manual effort".

"Do we have clear agreements with suppliers regarding planning horizons?"

"What do you mean exactly?"

"In which horizon, based on our forecasts, the suppliers already procure components, prepare semi-finished products, build stocks to overcome capacity bottlenecks or simply reserve capacities. In other words, at what point are we liable for these actions and until what week or month in the future are our forecasts merely non-binding outlooks that our suppliers can in turn use for their capacity planning, reservation of pre-products or settlement of procurement contracts?"

"I think we need to discuss this point in detail with the global procurement managers."

"Good, let's note down this action item and call it *Service Level Agreements* with suppliers. We should draft a proposal before approaching the procurement folks and later the suppliers. I suggest that we add these supplementary agreements to our procurement contracts at the latest with every new tender or when we change suppliers."

The conversation maintains this new positive mood as we continue talking. Finally, we agree that Ondrej and his team will invite the selected suppliers to short meetings to discuss the new way of working. The main point is that our partners understand why we are disclosing this data to them, how they can use it and what we expect in return. In my view, what we need to get from them is rough feedback on feasibility, that is, whether they have the manufacturing and logistics capacity or products in stock compared to our forecasts and can supply us on time and in the right quantities. Furthermore, I would expect that this would give us deeper understanding of our suppliers. Thus, if necessary, we also could jointly coordinate topics such as pre-production, postponements or breaking of demand peaks.

My minimum standard for the team is that we go through this process of sharing forecasts and obtaining feedback once a month, synchronised with the long-term capacity evaluations of our production lines. I'm aware that we will have a time lag as we cannot clarify all conditions externally as well as internally in the same planning week. However, since this is a rolling process, repeated monthly, I don't see this as critical and I'm convinced that we can continue to process the information that may arrive too late in the next planning cycle, so to speak.

Before we end the meeting, I have one last question for Ondrej. This is to understand how he, as a manager, involves his direct reports in these kinds of investigations. Does he collect suggestions or even encourage his staff to motivate them for change?

"By the way, before our meeting, did you discuss today's topic with your team to get opinions or counter-suggestions?"

He shakes his head no.

11 - The S&OP Workshop

Last week was focused on preparations for our workshop with the sales organisations. Mike came over from Switzerland for a few days to work with Vladimir and me. Above all, we want to ensure the workshop participants that the central Supply Chain function and our plant are well aligned. A key focus topic has been the overall planning process. To underline its importance, my team and I presented what we've learned in the previous months. Afterwards, Mike, Vladimir and I conceptualised the findings and suggestions. We call that concept "Sales and Operations Planning" and it will be the centre piece of the agenda. On the last day of what I considered to be successful preparation, I invited Mike to our home for dinner. Sophia prepared a delicious meal, and we ended the evening with a nice glass of Spanish red wine.

This morning, unfortunately, I don't have time to have breakfast with Sophia. I need to leave the flat shortly after 6:00 a.m. to be well prepared and less stressed for the big day. When Sophia hears me packing my office stuff, she quickly comes out of the bedroom to wish me a great conference. During the drive to the office, I repeatedly think through our concept and the corresponding practical examples. The rest of the commute I distract myself with my favourite music to get into a positive mood.

Two hours later, I greet Mike again, who was picked up from the airport by Marek. We meet with Vladimir and make sure that the meeting room, the necessary equipment and we ourselves are prepared for the coming event. Soon we'll be welcoming around thirty-five colleagues from various European branches of our company.

It's almost 10:00 and I look at the road that passes by the factory. Here it comes, the organised coach with our guests. Vladimir and I go outside to the security checkpoint to greet our visitors. To speed up the check-in, we have already provided name lists and safety shoes as well as the necessary clothing for the production tour planned for later in the day. As a result, everyone passes the security check quite quickly. On the way to the meeting room, I make some small talk and I'm very happy to see some familiar faces again, but also to meet several colleagues in person for the first time. Then everything goes quite quickly.

After coffee and finger food, Vladimir, Mike and I stand in front of today's audience and kick off the workshop. Pieter also joins us for the initial part, as he will introduce the factory and its role in the production network. We also present the full agenda:

- Introduction of participants and expectations
- Workshop objectives
- Presentation of the factory
- New planning concept
- Discussion on improvements in demand planning
- Plant tour
- Agreement on actions and next steps
- Evening programme in Prague with the planning team.

The conference is going well, and most participants contribute actively. I'm satisfied because we receive positive feedback about the latest development. This is extra motivation, which I will be happy to share with my team later on, because this contradicts the complaints I've heard internally about the lack of progress.

After a break, we get to the core of the workshop: the planning concept. We explain the need for an integrated, aligned and monthly recurring planning across different corporate functions. An important goal must be to use "one plan" as the basis for operational management of our supply chain, but also for financial purposes such as annual budget planning. We are not short of examples. We present to the participants many insights from the last few months. We explain the broken links between forecasting sales, long-term production planning and our supplier orders. We also point out the financial consequences if we wrongly plan capacities based on corrupt master data or enrich our product costing with inaccurate efficiency assumptions. In both cases, we often calculate manufacturing and product costs that deviate significantly from reality, leading to incorrect profit assumptions, sales pricing or even sales initiatives that are unfavourable for the company's success.

In passing, we also address the well-intentioned manipulation of demand plans. We underline our hypothesis of built-in security volumes, seemingly non-need-based or buffer-based sales forecasts, with examples we saw during a machine rebuild or relocation within our production network.

After these many points, we allow a brief discussion so that we can ensure the majority of our colleagues have understood the issues we've just presented. Now that we seem to have succeeded, we can move on to the theory. We've lined up several large flipcharts on one wall of our meeting room – representing one big page. Vladimir takes a thick felt-tip pen, draws a large circle in the middle of the page and signals with an arrow that this reflects a repetitive process. In the middle of the circle Mike writes "Integrated/Aligned Sales and Operations Planning". Together we fill-in the various steps around the circle:

1. Demand Planning (start)
2. Review / Confirmation of demand plan
3. Supply Planning (in our case production planning)
4. Review / Confirmation of supply plan
5. Demand and Supply reconciliation
6. Plans signed-off by management team (end).

We divide the audience into three groups and point to the assigned breakout rooms.

Mike will take over the first group and will talk about demand planning. His talk will include Pieter's lesson during our darts game. He will demonstrate that we can calculate with *precision* our sales plans whilst forecasting. Then variation could be buffered by inventories, lead time reductions from component procurement to customer order or reactive capacities. However, we will only ever understand the *accuracy* of the forecast once we see the actual sales (and thus know the target). This underlines the need to be well aligned with Sales and Marketing. We need to better understand the commercial activities, for example, promotions or advertising, customer agreements, competitor activities as well as adjustments to the product portfolio. This will enable a better understanding of sales risks and opportunities and result in the right corrective actions on the supply side. Mike will also touch on examples regarding macro data such as weather or consumer behaviour that could influence our forecasts. He will emphasise the point that a sales forecast should only be based on real customer demand; it should not include buffers and it must be adjusted for outliers. Losses due to supply shortages or other special events must be corrected or excluded from the calculation of forecasts.

Lastly, Mike will draw attention to the review and confirmation of the demand forecast. This is where the demand planners, who usually report to the Supply Chain, present any relevant changes and supporting analyses of their forecasting to Sales, Marketing and Controlling. This is to ensure that all assumptions, activities and influences for the coming months are taken into account. Our ambition to have a rolling plan for at least the next eighteen months is also addressed. In other words, we have to plan beyond one financial year. Of course, the further ahead we plan, the accuracy may decrease, so the downstream supply chain functions must be adaptable and flexible.

I take over the second group and guide them through the topic of Supply Planning. First, I explain the great variety of sub-processes in this area. Activities such as production planning, capacity planning, material call-off, import & export control, or deployment planning can be found in this scope of responsibility.

I also talk about the three dimensions of Supply Planning. Firstly, *time*: execution of very short-term tasks such as a to-the-minute detailed production schedule or day-by-day delivery schedule to various warehouses to multi-year simulations as the basis for investment projects. Also, *place*: coordination of material flows with local suppliers to international procurement or sales processes. Finally, *products*: consideration of the end-product through all sub-processes, like semi-finished products to individual components.

In simplified terms, the forecasts from demand planning are converted into a delivery, production or procurement plan. To do this, the planner takes into account the different lead times for material movements in the logistics network or process time for various production stages as well as order lead times when purchasing required raw or packaging materials. Existing inventories across all supply chain locations and production stages are also considered as well as available capacities. For the rolling planning concept, I emphasise that supply planning must also be executed over a longer horizon. Medium-term capacity planning with the help of Rough-Cut Capacity Plans is the heart of the reconciliation between demand and supply plans. Among other things, this is where we evaluate whether we can pre-produce, increase capacities or outsource production.

Finally, I explain the different types of stock. Safety Stock covers supply and demand fluctuations and can be differentiated seasonally. Cycle Stock, on the other hand, reflects the batch size or frequency in production. Contingency or Project Stock can be used during crises or events such as the relocation of production lines. Transit Stock depends on the means of transport used for shipping and distance, i.e., transit-time (overseas: many weeks; domestic: a few hours or days by truck). Process Stocks represent quarantine for quality controls or customs inspections and are to be defined depending on the product characteristics or control requirements of the individual product. They can cover a few hours to several days. Stocks can exist along the total value chain in the form of components, semi-finished or finished products. I conclude by pointing out that we can redefine the inventory logic by considering opportunities and risks related to our planning via the monthly process.

Vladimir discusses with the third group the reconciliation of the plans as well as the acceptance of the plan by the management. He roughly summarises relevant points made by Mike and me and explicitly addresses the management decisions needed in these two process steps. In capacity planning, for example, it may come out that we have insufficient goods in stock because we cannot produce enough. This would lead to supply gaps against the sales forecast and our customers would be affected by delivery shortfalls and may become dissatisfied. Such insights, feedback and transparency relating to the opportunities and risks of the plan are the essential core of the planning concept. If necessary, forecasts must be corrected. This can take the form of postponing promotions or offering substitute products. On the other hand, the management could decide to accept higher costs and raise capital to procure products externally, invest in additional capacities or simply increase inventory. Opportunities and risks can also occur in the form of production output variation, price changes in the procurement of components, new sales possibilities or customer losses in the selling countries. Once management agrees on the plan, it should not only be executed within the supply chain but also taken into account in the company's financial and commercial planning.

After half an hour each, we rotate the teams through the different topics and breakout rooms so that by the end everyone has covered and hopefully fully understood all six steps of the "Sales and Operations Planning" process. Back in the large meeting room, the participants receive a handout with key points for process success. After a break, we discuss and agree with all participants on the introduction of the planning concept and create a binding action plan for its implementation and regular monitoring. The main responsibility will be taken by Mike's central planning team, and he will conduct internal audits for the largest markets in the coming months to confirm process compliance and outline needed improvements. We also offer monthly "question and answer" meetings to quickly resolve any issues.

After we've worked through all the agenda items and our colleagues are on the bus back to Prague, Vladimir, Mike and I high-five each other. We made a good team. Vladimir and I also interacted well together, and nobody would have suspected our differences of opinion. I'm glad that we represented our factory well and I'm confident that the meeting participants will travel back to their markets with a positive conclusion. Now I'm looking forward to a relaxing, social evening in the city.

We meet in one of my favourite restaurants, the Brasileiro. It offers enough space for large groups, a first-class selection of diverse dishes and both the atmosphere and the service are excellent. My team leaders, Jana, Magdalena and Ondrej, but also Leos, who keeps close contact with the country planners, join us in the restaurant and mingle with the guests. There is a lot of laughter and good conversation. My team and our guests seem to be enjoying themselves, even a smaller group continues the evening with a bit of sightseeing in the city. The convivial atmosphere helps to forget any disputes between colleagues. I have high hopes that it will help us to have a fresh start and ease some of the more difficult business relationships.

Hitting home, I find Sophia already asleep. After having a shower, I fall into bed well after midnight, exhausted but with a big smile on my face.

12 - Creating a Future-proof Team

Weeks later, I'm still buoyed by the workshop's success. The number of production non-deliveries is continuously decreasing, inventories have stabilised at desired levels and the relations within the factory between production and my team are excellent. The trend is our friend, and it motivates me greatly to move forward with these successes that can act as tailwinds.

I drive onto the factory premises to the parking space assigned to me. As I get out of my car, I hear a vehicle driving by along the road with loud, electronic music. Shortly afterwards the music becomes quieter, but I can still make it out. It's Pieter in his sports car. He has turned the music down as he passes the gate. As he gets out, I wish him a good morning and ask about the music. He calls out the name of the artist and winks at me. I smile with a surprised look on my face because I like this kind of music too and didn't imagine that someone Pieter's age would still listen loudly to trance music. We walk together to the office building. As we say goodbye, he says, "Today I'll solve one of your problems. Come to my office at 11:00!" Astonished, I watch him walk away and then start my workday. During the first few appointments, I can't really concentrate because all my thoughts circle around Pieter's statement. What could he possibly have meant by that? Fortunately, I don't have to struggle with my curiosity for too long as the time of our meeting comes around quickly.

On time, I go to the second floor where Pieter's office is located. As soon as I leave the stairs, I hear Pieter arguing loudly. His assistant indicates that I should take a seat in front of his office. The discussion seems to be all over the place, and I only make out individual words behind the closed door. Now I also perceive the second voice: it's Vladimir sitting in Pieter's office! I get nervous, bite my lips and don't know where to put my hands. I suspect what is happening, but before I can complete my thinking process, the door flies open. Vladimir stomps energetically and red-faced out of the room. I imagine that he has noticed me out of the corner of his eye. He ignores me and rushes out of the lobby. Pieter's assistant looks at me, shocked and wordless. We both know what has just happened: Vladimir has just been dismissed.

A few minutes later, I'm sitting in front of Pieter with a glass of water in my hand. Contrary to my usually energetic nature, I'm calm and silent. I knew this day would come eventually – here and there I was looking forward to it. It was supposed to increase my decision-making freedom, responsibility and also remove nasty internal conflict. But sitting in Pieter's office makes me feel like I share Vladimir's fate. I don't feel satisfaction or even slight success. On the contrary, I feel sorry for Vladimir. We've worked well together over the past few weeks and we've both made a real effort. He has even started sharing personal stories about his family and opened himself to me. Pieter interrupts my guilty thoughts. You can literally feel his detachment and many years of experience as he makes me understand that this is quite a normal procedure in management roles. As if nothing has happened, he congratulates me on my wider responsibility as the warehouse and transport departments are now also under my supervision. Then he gets serious again, leans over the desk and looks at me sharply.

"Are there any other personal issues in your team?"

Surprised, I ask him what he means by that.

"Don't be like that! I'm talking about whether you have employees in the team with whom we should end the cooperation here and now."

I'm aware of what he is getting at, but I'm trying to gain time because everything is moving too fast for me right now. I'm a young manager and have not yet experienced many reorganisations. When I realise how serious he is, I give him insights into my current thinking. I tell him about Ondrej and that I don't agree with his leadership style, and that he doesn't take any of my advice or hints positively. Of all things, I'm bothered by the little trust we have been able to build and the arrogance he expresses towards me. I outline the possibilities of far-reaching changes in the team that could be initiated in case of him leaving the plant. Pieter listens carefully and advises me to go to HR today and prepare Ondrej's termination contract. He justifies the speed by saying that my team and especially the logistics functions, which will now also be my responsibility, may be worried as soon as they understand that Vladimir is no longer there. So, I should seize the opportunity and clear the air, so that in the coming months no further uncertainties arise due to personnel decisions and the team regains trust and stability soon. Before we end our conversation, he wishes me well for the upcoming difficult talk with Ondrej and advises me not to talk about these changes with the team any further today. I should first sleep after today's events and process my emotions. Tomorrow is another day when I can openly disclose all the changes to the team.

After the conversation, I gather all my courage and sneak to Vladimir's office. I knock once, twice, three times – no response. I open the door and realise that he took all his personal belongings and is already gone. We didn't get to say goodbye to each other. Maybe it's better that way because I imagine he perceives the current situation as a personal attack and would not be very interested in talking to me.

The discussion with HR and Ondrej goes quickly. I'm surprisingly unemotional and settled during our face-to-face discussion. I feel as if I'm fast-forwarding a movie. Ondrej's reaction is as expected. He doesn't understand our points and denies I'm on the right track with the initiated changes. His feedback and behaviour confirm the plan to release him of his duties with immediate effect and work with the team understaffed for a few weeks. For me, this event gives an important lesson for the future: It's necessary to remove toxic people, even if they may have the most experience in the team. This is the only way to avoid poisoning the whole team in the long run, to avoid negative effects on their mood, motivation and willingness to change.

As I enter the open-plan office late in the afternoon, it's clear to me that every single one of my colleagues senses that something has happened. I don't know if Ondrej said anything at all, and if so, what he said when leaving. I briefly stand in the middle of the room and tell everyone that I will make an announcement tomorrow morning during our daily status updates. The team leader in charge of the warehouse is also attending the meeting, so I can outline background here as well. Pieter has also told me not to disclose any details, but only to point out the necessity of the change and to thank Vladimir and Ondrej for their commitment. There will be official information about it anyway. I should calmly point out my idea for a general structural change with regards to the sub-teams. The reasoning is clear, and I can easily back it up. After all, we want to create a future-proof team, progress on the journey we have started and continuously improve our results.

At dinner I tell Sophia about my eventful day. She notices that I'm still tense and emotionally battered. I'm grateful for her attempts to distract me. After watching a movie, I enjoy an extensive massage. Still, I can't fall asleep for a long time. She lies on my chest, and I can feel her heartbeat. It seems like she's already sleeping. I briefly consider waking her up to demand some further distraction. But I don't want to be too selfish, so I close my eyes and start to concentrate on my breath and let my thoughts drift. In such moments, where I cannot calm down, I always imagine sitting on a bench looking up at the blue sky. Each cloud that passes by represents a thought. I notice the cloud – the thought – but let it move on without spending too much time on it. This kind of meditation needs practice, and unfortunately, I don't always succeed in applying it. It takes a while, but at some point, I fall asleep.

13 - Reorganising for a Performance Boost

The last few weeks have been marked by uncertainty within my team. Many staff members were frightened by what they saw as unforeseen personnel changes and worried about their jobs or scope of responsibilities. Our management team was not immune to this either. The last meetings were more taciturn than usual and hardly anyone dared to offer even constructive criticism of Pieter's impulses and plans.

I particularly dislike the distance that suddenly exists between individual members of the site leadership team and me. As I expatriated from the head office, I again feel they have reservations about my motivation and agenda. There is less open communication happening and it feels like they are avoiding interactions. Of course, Pieter and I get along well, and I appreciate him as a supervisor, but above all as a coach. But everyone should have noticed by now that I don't get any special treatment and that my performance is judged strictly. Anyhow, it feels like an additional burden, and I hope to regain the trust of my colleagues soon. Ultimately, my openness and constant bias for action should contribute positively to this.

At least the dust seems to finally be settling within my department. I've had many personal conversations. I've tried to listen to the fears and concerns of the employees, but I've also revealed my vision and motivation once again. I've attempted to make clear that my intention is to work for our factory for a longer time and I only want to move on once we have become one of the best locations in terms of customer service and supply chain planning. I also like living in Prague very much and have come to appreciate many of my colleagues.

Above all, the development of the employees is close to my heart, and I want to positively contribute to advancing their skillset. The first successes are visible to everyone in the example of Leos. This is well supported with positive feedback from key stakeholders and customers. Through the many conversations I've had, I've gained some insights that were previously hidden from me. For example, the struggle to balance short-term operational with tasks of tactical nature like managing product change projects or long-term supplier relationships but also some work preferences of team members. I can and will use these for the upcoming organisational adjustments. I clearly communicated on the day after Vladimir was let go that there would be no further dismissals for the time being. But it has also been indicated that we'll make some minor adjustments to the organisation, in the form of reviewing the roles of individual staff members including their scope of responsibility. The objective is to be better aligned with a holistic and end-to-end supply chain planning approach. These reorganisations shall also strengthen the execution of our monthly planning concept.

The bigger challenge is to communicate with the team lead of our warehouse operations. She has been Vladimir's right hand so far. Jana, as well as my colleagues from the management team, have made it clear to me that she manages the various warehouse locations and related workforce well. I also don't want to create any further challenges. When I consult with HR and plant Controlling, I'm told that no urgent areas for action have been identified here. So, I can continue to focus on coordinating the suppliers and our production, as well as further polishing the external image of our factory.

Under these circumstances, I decide to maintain the status quo within logistics for the time being. However, one small change is necessary. I have not yet managed to attend the Czech language classes. Well, to be more precise, after the first few lessons, I've been avoiding further lessons and using the stress at work as an excuse. To be honest, speaking and writing Czech is harder for me than I thought. Even individual words are so puzzling and do not make sense to me. For example, the word for ice cream is *zmrzlina*. I simply can't remember these hard-to-pronounce words, not to mention the grammar. Maybe I just lack motivation. You don't have to know and be able to do everything, I try to tell myself. Sophia, on the other hand, already speaks several languages and has a good understanding of them, thanks to her Latin certificate. She is eager to learn Czech, and I'm always thrilled when she holds a short dialogue in the local language in a shop or restaurant.

But let's get back to my real problem: I can't talk to the forklift drivers, order pickers and other warehouse workers in person. Not even with their group leader. They don't speak English and I don't understand Czech either. Therefore, so far, I've asked Jana or sometimes Magdalena to accompany me to help translating. But this leads to losing the personal touch and the nuances of a message. Consequently, I decided to entrust Jana with a new role in the department. She is already my "right-hand" anyway, so it is a good fit that I now place the majority of the department's staff under her supervision. For her, this also provides a further development opportunity. In the future, she will manage about thirty-five employees and can thus build up experience and knowledge in the field of warehouse and transport logistics. At first, I thought that the group leader might take this move as a demotion. But several conversations confirmed that this change also benefits her. She can take care of a variety of continuous improvement measures in our logistics processes while Jana relieves her of some management tasks and, above all, in Jana she has a new supervisor and deputy with whom she can exchange ideas in an understandable and personal way. Since I maintain an "open door" culture, she can of course approach me directly at any time - with language assistance, of course.

Jana has been of great help during these difficult weeks. She was the first person on-site with whom I talked confidentially about the planned changes and also my own feelings. We exchanged ideas and reviewed the individual employee profiles to talk through strengths, weaknesses, motivation, knowledge gaps and development potential. I am under the impression that she understands my idea of supply chain management: "Logistics, Procurement and Production are the necessary building blocks that all producing companies need - Planning, on the other hand, is where one can shine and differentiate". Therefore, we are well aligned in our vision but still have fruitful arguments on the alternative routes to get there.

What I value most, apart from Jana's trustworthiness, honesty and her discretion on confidential topics, is that she shares well-founded criticism or feedback with me. She reflects on my behaviour or the reactions it triggers in the team - both negative and positive. I find this immensely important, especially as a young manager. Otherwise, it's easy to get into the habit of having characteristics that, in the long run, create little enthusiasm within one's team but also among peers. In the end, Pieter's tip to quickly find a person I could trust within the team paid off. I hope that Jana also perceives our professional relationship as enriching.

The final organisation of my department is now in place. In addition to Jana, who is responsible for physical logistics, Magdalena is in charge of production planning and Jakub, materials planning. Jakub's previous task of transport and export planning will be integrated into logistics, Jana's team. This will further streamline the number of my direct reports. There will be no differentiation of the teams according to product portfolio anymore. In my mind, products simply have different characteristics or are manufactured on different equipment. From a process point of view, I would like to avoid differences in planning for product categories and enable better temporary replacements within the sub-teams during holidays or larger projects. The same applies to material planning.

I like the idea that the team leaders also perform operational tasks and are an active part of the process chain for which they are responsible. In order to support our rolling planning process, which we started a while ago at the big workshop, the tasks in production and material planning are differentiated according to planning horizons and clearly defined. The team leaders take responsibility for the medium- to long-term planning horizon, including relevant projects, and are thus the link to demand planning of individual markets. The team members are more concerned with the short-term - and thus, very operational - horizon of approximately the next three months with a focus on production, warehouses or suppliers. We have created detailed job descriptions and training materials to clearly differentiate the positions. Of course, we also assigned appropriate job titles and conducted a skills analysis involving staff to identify knowledge or skill gaps to address them over the next few months.

In this context, we did not fill Ondrej's position as a manager but recruited an additional production planner. In the end, we gave a career changer the chance to complete our team. I didn't want to train a production employee to be a planner, but rather looked for someone who could take a neutral stance. The focus in the recruitment was on good analytical skills as well as an excellent ability to handle and interpret large amounts of data. Through a small case study, we tested how good the candidate's intuition is in dealing with uncertainties and decision-making when relevant data is not available.

I'm happy with the changes and hope these will result in further boosting our performance to achieve the proclaimed ambitions.

14 – Think Big: Best Supply Chain Team

It's the weekend. Sophia and I are sitting in the living room, planning a short trip to visit my family. Whilst doing so, we wander further in time to the family celebration at Lake Constance, to a wedding in central Germany and a couple of visitors who will join us for a city weekend in Prague. Finally, we take a calendar, mark the dates and compare them to our holiday planning. This exercise triggers a professional thought. Normally we avoid talking about work on weekends, but I dare to make an exception.

"Tell me, Sophia, what kind of goal setting technique, like regular status updates and monitoring, did you like best from your previous supervisors?"

She looks at me frowning and I explain again what I'm after: I'm looking for a concept that can be used to capture relevant goals, but above all the most important prerequisites for achieving them. I add that I'm less interested in tracking key figures than in recording the medium- to long-term measures that will ultimately contribute to sustainable goal achievement.

"Now I follow you. My last boss used some kind of matrix in our monthly departmental meetings. I can't remember the name, but didn't you cover these topics in your business economist studies?"

"That's a good idea. I'll look for my course materials in the basement."

In the cellar, there are several unpacked boxes. In the box labelled "Study material", I quickly find what I'm looking for and take the documents on "leadership and management" upstairs. One coffee later, I've found the relevant theory.

"Is it possible that your boss used a tool called Balanced Scorecard?"

"Exactly, that was the title of the table on the office notice board."

I read through the theory for a while and have to admit to myself that I've already forgotten most of it. On a sheet of paper, I draw four large quadrants, two in the upper and two in the lower half, so it looks like a four-field matrix. I label the box at the top left "financial or business perspective" and the one next to it "customer perspective". In the bottom half I write "internal process perspective" on the left and "learning and development perspective" on the right.

I search the internet and find some good websites on the subject as well as one or two videos in which practising managers talk about their application of the matrix. One of the videos talks about an interesting concept. Here the letter "Z" is written in large letters over the four fields. Because of the arrowhead in the field "financial perspective", I notice that this is not supposed to represent a letter as such, but a large, but twisted arrow. One website gives a catchy explanation for this, they call it Theory Z: If employees have the right skills and are highly motivated, then they will initiate as well as implement necessary process changes. This, in turn, leads to better results with internal or external customers, ensuring the achievement of overall business goals. I realise that this is a very simple presentation. In any case, the connections seem convincing to me. It is also generalised in such a way that I hope to be able to put my department's objectives into a good structure and also implement them effectively with the team.

Sophia interrupts my thought process and indicates it's time to leave because we wanted to go to the zoo today. Before we set off, I send my team leaders an invitation for the coming week for a brainstorming session on our objectives.

A few days later, Jana, Magdalena, Jakub and I are sitting together. I seem to have succeeded in explaining the concept around the Balanced Scorecard, the Theory Z especially has fallen on fertile ground. We have four flipcharts distributed around the room, each reflecting one of the perspectives of the matrix. Each of us holds sticky notes and a pen. I outline the framework for our collection of ideas with the motto "Best supply chain team in the production network". Furthermore, I add that many small ideas and improvement measures, accumulated over a longer period of time, can lead to big changes. Therefore, every idea, whether minor or already created during the last months of our cooperation, should be included.

After about twenty minutes, I notice how the frequency of note-taking decreases. We stop the brainstorming and review the collected points flipchart by flipchart. Meanwhile, we cluster similar or identical contributions and ask clarification questions when necessary. In the end, we have collected a balanced but long list of topics. For the "internal process perspective" we accumulated by far the most ideas. According to my research, this is also to be expected and therefore not unusual. Here we find measures such as the implementation of our new monthly rolling planning concept or the alignment of planning parameters between Production, Controlling and our team.

I particularly like the fact that we had some ideas in the first quadrant around the topic of "learning & development". Here, for example, we find the development of a skills matrix for our differentiated planning jobs and that we want to organise a monthly kind of "coffee & learn" interaction. The idea behind this is that one or two employees present a topic that is relevant to their job. In this way, we can continue our internal education in a pleasant atmosphere and gain new insights into other topics.

In the "customer perspective" quadrant we've included the idea of an internal customer satisfaction survey. Here we want to ask other departments in our factory, but also our international customers, in a standardised way what we are good at from their perspective and what potential there is for improvement. With an annual comparison of the survey results, we could then check progress and identify new areas for development.

On the flipchart of the "financial perspective" are typical key figures such as cost and savings targets.

We agree that I will initially fill in the Balanced Scorecard based on our preliminary work. At the next team meeting we'll review the content and priorities. As soon as we're aligned internally, we'll present the matrix to Mike in the head office as well as to the plant leadership team. After all, we'll need support in the form of advice, resources or even willingness to change from many different departments or functions. Of course, we also want to make sure that our ambitions are in line with the overall company goals of the head office as well as my line manager. Finally, we'll inform the rest of our Supply Chain team and determine the objectives for the personnel performance evaluation cycle for the current year, but also for the new year, from the Balanced Scorecard. We'll mark the monthly progress of the individual measures with a simple traffic light like colour system – this requires measurable intermediate steps and a timetable for implementation.

15 - The Supply Review

Hastily, I sprint up the stairs and open the door to the meeting room, out of breath. Magdalena has already kicked off the meeting and I unintentionally interrupt her presentation. All my colleagues turn to the door and a sly smile slips across my face. Pieter shakes his head, and I can literally hear his thoughts: "Young man, are you ever going to get to a meeting on time?" I take a seat without comment and put my notebook on the table. If I had dared to attempt an apology or excuse now, I would have handed Pieter on a plate an opportunity for one of his amusingly direct yet instructive lessons. I'll spare myself that today because I'm now sitting with the factory's management team in the meeting I invite them to every month - our Sales and Operations Planning meeting. This approximately two-hour-long meeting is the result of our monthly planning concept and was realised directly after the successful workshop. We always meet in the third week of the month to align on the plant's demand forecast, our capacities, portfolio changes as well as production and inventory planning.

As Magdalena is now in charge of all production planning, she prepares the presentation content and leads the meetings. In addition to the agenda items already mentioned, Jakub will join us later and give us an outlook on raw material and packaging material supply. For this, he uses feedback received from our suppliers after sharing our long-term material plans. He sometimes also obtains insights from our central procurement department.

We usually start with a short review of the factory's key performance indicators. We discuss customer service, the production efficiencies achieved and the plan fulfilment over the past period, look at the loss rates and obsolescence costs and close with our stock band adherence (min/max) for components as well as finished goods. We've learned that we need to focus on reviewing a longer-term planning horizon. In the first meetings, we only talked about short-term and tangible events, and so we had to admit that we, as managers, were too concerned with operational issues. We decided our aim in these meetings should be to make tactical decisions at an early stage or give reliable feedback to the head office or customers on the fulfilment of their needs. In order to select the right time horizons, we looked at, for example, what lead times are needed to increase or decrease shift patterns, procure components without forecast or realise smaller investments. In our case, we agreed that especially the period after the fourth month should be in focus. In addition, we should look ahead at least the next twelve months, at best even eighteen months. Thus, we also cover planning periods relevant for financial planning, such as an annual plan or quarterly updates, and we can try to use the plan approved in the reconciliation meetings as a basis for financial planning.

After we have discussed the capacities for the next one and a half years and cleared up a misunderstanding with the head of engineering about the maintenance plan, it's my turn. Magdalena is already projecting my explanatory slide. It shows a complex structure with various ramifications and percentages. It is a loss tree that is supposed to break down our service and delivery problems. Pieter assigned me this task in the last meeting because, although he is satisfied with the positive trend in our service levels, that is, on-time and in-full adherence to our customer orders, we are still below the target value of 98.5 per cent required by the head office.

I take the meeting participants through the individual loss tree branches, for example:

- Missing packaging or raw material
- Significant deviations in demand plans
- Undifferentiated and incorrectly calculated safety stocks
- Production shortfall in output compared to plan
- Major production line breakdowns
- Wrong inventory balance in the warehouse, or
- System errors that cause machine idle time.

We will re-do this loss tree again in a few months to evaluate whether the magnitudes of the different loss tree branches have changed. Consistently recording such data is desirable, but difficult to do without systematic support.

On the subject of safety stocks, I explain the calculation formula we have chosen and go into the sometimes embarrassing findings. We often wonder why we have various supply failures. In fact, we calculate with the wrong parameters in the formula. This can be, for example, a wrongly chosen process cycle time. If an article is only produced once a quarter, I expect at least that long a lead time in the calculation as part of the mathematical safety stock formula. But worse, however, are management decisions to achieve inventory reductions. In the past, a safety stock was given, say, six weeks. But if the properly performed calculation now gives eight weeks, this means that we change the parameters of the equation and may not achieve the intended service target (98.5 per cent in this case). I give more examples on the flipchart and write down some equations for better visual understanding.

Another point is immediately noticeable and there are questions from colleagues about it: demand planning or orders from our customers. I explain that about every second delivery failure can be attributed to insufficient demand planning. I'm even convinced that in the future three out of four service failures will result from unplanned, high demand fluctuations. The focus on sales forecasting will need to increase once we have managed to optimise our material and production planning.

We again shift focus and talk through examples of last-minute changes in demand plans or customer requests to which we were unable to respond. Furthermore, I explain that due to insufficient forecast accuracy we often produce the wrong products. We chase inflated forecasts across the broad product portfolio of our sales organisations. Therefore, we may falsely allocate capacity or consume shared components mistakenly, which may be missing for a more important production order later in the cycle.

A good discussion ensues, and we try to understand what possibilities there are to offer our customers increased flexibility or better responsiveness (so they stop inflating their forecasts). For a while, we get stuck on the topic of "reactive capacities" and discuss possible solutions to enable the build-up of an additional capacity and material buffer for our main production lines. This could, in turn, be used in the short term for emergency production for customer requests that need to be prioritised. We agree to go through this issue in detail with a smaller group later this week. Eventually, Pieter interrupts the energetic discussion and looks at me.

"Do you have an evaluation of which countries have the biggest discrepancies between their actual sales and forecast?"

"We have prepared such a report. Magdalena, please go ahead to the corresponding slide in the presentation."

We show the more than twenty-five countries that are supplied by our factory. For this we use a simple Pareto diagram. Here it quickly becomes clear which countries account for the major share of absolute forecast deviations. Pieter seems satisfied and leans forward.

"If I understand it correctly, our German organisation represents the main challenge. Gabriel, what do you intend to do about it?"

"Well, I have already discussed the situation with Mike. As you know, the national companies always have their demand reviews the week before our supply review meeting. Our German colleagues are now also holding these meetings. Mike told me that none of our sister plants is satisfied with the demand planning quality from Hamburg."

"Ok, but what do we do concretely about it? After all, there are regular complaints from exactly that sales organisation about our delivery performance. I don't want this to happen any longer!"

"One suggestion would be for Mike and me to travel to one of their local demand review meetings. Being there in person, we could learn how the meetings are run and make kind of an internal audit. After that, it should certainly be possible to identify improvement measures. I'm just not sure if they would want us to attend this meeting. After all, this is integrated into their monthly board meeting."

"There won't be an obstacle. I'll call the managing director in Hamburg today, so go ahead and book your trip. In our next meeting, I expect you to come up with tangible actions to be implemented by the sales organisations to ensure a higher quality input into the plans we steer our factory with."

16 – The Demand Review

Three weeks later, I'm waiting for a taxi at Hamburg airport. Mike couldn't come after all, as he had already planned another business trip. So, I'll go alone to the shark tank, that is, the German board meeting. As soon as next week, Pieter is expecting constructive feedback on how to improve demand planning. While driving through the city, I look out of the window to get a glimpse of the city. I'm glad I'm staying overnight, and hopefully, the weather will remain good so that I can stroll through the city in the evening. The historic warehouse district "Speicherstadt", in particular, is supposed to be worth a visit.

The taxi stops in front of the towering, modern office building. There is a world of difference between visiting a factory and a head office that is home to Sales and Marketing. The building has modern offices, floor-to-ceiling windows with a flood of daylight. The reception alone looks inviting and makes you want to work here. Of course, fewer customers or other business partners visit a production facility. But I'm still a little jealous when I think about what these luxurious offices have to offer, from top canteen catering to a fitness studio. Looking around, I imagine that every euro we save in the factory is spent here to polish up the company's external image. Also, the staff is dressed completely differently - everybody seems to wear suits. At our factory, you would be overdressed showing up like that. Only when an important supplier or a customer delegation comes to visit do we dress that way. Personally, I like the business casual style much better - more individuality and more reality than illusion. But let's leave such thoughts aside. After all, I don't want to be negatively biased during the upcoming Demand Review meeting.

Someone taps on my shoulder. I turn around. It's Marcel, the head of demand planning for the German-speaking sales region. He greets me in a friendly manner and invites me for a coffee. After all, we have almost an hour to spare before Sales & Operations is on the board meeting's agenda. We use this opportunity for a preliminary discussion. Marcel shares some insights and specifics, especially describing the characters of the VP of sales and the head of marketing. Both play an essential role in the Demand Review. I've already met the German managing director, Henning, at a workshop in Switzerland some time ago. He embodies the typical executive on the cover of a business magazine - tall, well-styled with an eloquent way of speaking. You can learn a lot from people like him, but personally, I prefer people like Pieter, who are outspoken, down-to-earth, and approachable.

It's time and we take the lift to the top floor. In front of us there is a large glass-walled meeting room. Once we are recognised, we are waved in. I unpack my documents and take a seat. After the current agenda item has been closed, all eyes turn to me because Henning asks me for a short introduction of myself and the reason for the visit. The German management team looks a little incredulous at first, as I have already had so many career opportunities within our company in my mid-twenties and some can't quite believe it. A normal management trainee has normally only just completed his studies at my age and has had his first work assignment. Sometimes I wish I were a few years older, as this might give me more seniority without having to prove my knowledge or skills every time.

After presenting my CV and the motivation for improving our planning process, I'm asked to briefly say a few words about our plant and its current challenges. I directly take the opportunity to explain the context and importance of an integrated and well aligned planning process, using short and clear examples. I go into the initiatives we have already implemented and show why we are dissatisfied with the quality of demand planning from our receiving markets. To underline this statement, I re-use the service loss tree and the Pareto diagram from our last factory Supply Review meeting, which shows that we need much better forecast accuracy leading to less demand volatility.

A few minutes later, Marcel presents the current demand planning insights. For this, he gives a summary of his team's sales forecasts. In order to translate the data for board members, the individual stock-keeping unit, or SKU, data has been grouped on brands and assortments but also matched to the relevant sales/distribution channels. We are currently looking at the products that are mostly produced in our factory. The projected sales of these items are shown in tonnes. Marcel shows the coming twelve months and compares them both in annual total and in monthly phasing compared to the same period of last year. This makes it easy to recognise any deviations between the periods in terms of seasonality or also in promotional volumes. However, since the forecast covers a period beyond the fiscal year, subtotals are also shown for the current financial year. These are then a mixture of already realised sales and the forecast, that is, the anticipated sales.

Marcel keeps trying to bring the commercial heads into play and invites comments on his data. Ultimately, the objective is to understand the opportunities and risks of the plan he presents and to agree on specific adjustments in the demand plans before they are sent to the factories and suppliers.

During Marcel's attempts to trigger a discussion, I have to smile inwardly. The descriptions he gave me earlier of the roles and characteristics of the people were spot on. The marketing manager is rather cool and tactical. She knows a lot about portfolio changes and campaigns. She can thus comment well, nevertheless only superficially. The sales manager's word is most important. He seems to like the sound of his own voice and I find it difficult to understand the point of his long remarks. Actually, I would now expect Henning, in his role as managing director, to step in and demand clear statements and conclusions. But this does not happen. I remain quiet not to interfere - I'll only provide feedback at the end of the meeting.

The sales manager doesn't share much insight but still provides an answer, or rather an excuse, for all the questions. Marcel tries to stress the critical points, especially where sales are below marketing expectations, or the trend is negative. Marcel also asks about positive deviations because he wants to understand whether a trend is confirmed or the reason for the additional sales. In the end, little light is shed on the situation and the VP of sales reacts with annoyance at some point. "How am I supposed to know what we'll sell in half a year? I don't own a crystal ball!" I find this statement interesting because as soon as Marcel presents figures that are lower than the financial targets, he immediately argues against how unrealistic these figures are and that his team will make up for the losses until the end of the fiscal year. There are no clear actions agreed - and again I wish the managing director would intervene and demand that they avoid this kind of sandbagging.

After an hour, Marcel finishes his presentation. I don't see any real action points on the flipchart nor properly outlined opportunities and risks. I wonder what he will do now with the information he gained from the meeting. Now it's my turn, and in confidence I step forward with my notepad in hand. I take a pen and start to write on the empty flipchart whilst commenting using my notes. Point by point, I explain what I've observed and how we'll move forward to ensure a better monthly Sales & Operations Planning meeting. I noticed that the commercial functions could do little with the planning unit, such as tonnes, pieces or litres. Only the head of finance was able to follow well here. Therefore, I suggest that we come up with a translation to convert from operational quantity data to financial data, such as sales revenue. In this context, we could divide the figures for the current financial year into "year to date" (sales revenue generated in the previous months) and "year to go" (sales revenue still to be generated until the end of the financial year). We will then compare these two key figures with the previous year and, above all, with the annual plan, that is, the budget. This will show whether the target achievement is still realistic at all.

This is where Henning's role comes into play. He should critically scrutinise the figures, data and facts in the meeting and ensure that it results in a realistic plan. Opportunities and risks do not always have to be reflected in the operational plan immediately, but they need to be communicated to the central Supply Chain function as well as the factories. In this way, Henning can also see whether the target achievement of his national company is at all achievable. He can intervene with corrective measures at an early stage and have them evaluated via the monthly planning process.

After a short discussion, I point out that no key figures at all have been discussed, such as customer delivery performance or, most importantly, the quality of the demand forecasts. We agree to work out a standard format for the KPI review. Finally, I explain again the need for a longer-term outlook. I give examples of which changes we can react to in the factories or with our upstream suppliers and which deviations from the plan are more likely to lead to difficulties and disappointed customers at the end of the day. Marcel and I explain how the meeting output, even not fully reflected in the operational plans, could be utilised for simulations. Later, we also talk about topics like "demand sensing" or "statistical forecasting". Here, too, we agree to work together with the head office to see what best practices exist within our network to automate demand planning and also to increase planning accuracy, especially in the medium- to long-term horizon. If necessary, we'll hire a consultant, as demand planning is an essential and important input into the company's supply chain, a bit like GIGO, garbage in, garbage out (the quality of output is determined by the quality of the input).

I leave it at these points. I decide not to go into the behavioural aspects of the meeting participants, as I lack the courage to do so. What do I have to offer these experienced managers? At the end of my summary, I receive appreciative nods and Henning's agreement that he will ensure the improvement actions are pursued. Nevertheless, I read between his lines that it will take a while to get accustomed to the new ways of working and there might be some setbacks along the way. I think: *Maybe we will need to repeat this kind of audit of the local processes soon*.

After we have left the room, Marcel thanks me for the support. "I've tried to make a difference here several times. I think it's been good for us to get your outside perspective and I hope our leaders will interact better with me in those meetings in the future."

Shortly after, I say goodbye and make my way to the hotel. After freshening up, I explore Hamburg on foot. On the way, I talk to Sophia on the phone and we tell each other about our day. Afterwards, I grab some takeaway and sit down by the water to admire the impressive and illuminated cargo cranes and anchored vessels.

17 - No Time to be Bored

Almost as suddenly as Pieter appeared as temporary plant director, he departed again. A fortnight ago, he told us that a new plant manager had been nominated by headquarters and that he would concentrate on his previous role as soon as possible. The management team already knows the name of his successor: Christoph, a Dutchman whom I had the opportunity to meet during one of my projects in Sweden. Until recently, he led a plant with similar production technologies in the Nordics. In a few days, he will join us and officially introduce himself.

This is exactly why the factory leadership team is sitting together right now. We are preparing Christoph's arrival and want to give him a first overview of our factory and current undertakings. For this purpose, we're preparing a presentation folder for Marek to take to the airport when he picks Christoph up so that he can read it on the way to Nelahozeves. In general, it can be said that the team is motivated and enthusiastic. The capital expenditures in our location have not stopped so far and the operational performance has been quite positive in recent months. In addition, there is a much better external image when talking to head office functions or the markets' sales organisations. The entire team is full of positive expectations and is looking forward to entering a phase of further stabilisation and increased efficiency - under Christoph's leadership. This is also very much needed after the exhausting crisis management of the past months. Looking around our group, I can see how much energy has been put into the implementation of various tasks. The pressure was enormous, and Pieter also regularly underlined the high expectations.

The only downer, which we address directly in the presentation, is the innovation flop that has unfortunately occurred with the vitamin shots. In the last quarter, we discontinued production due to a lack of consumer demand and have already had to lay off various production employees. The infrastructure fixed costs will be fully written off in the coming months. Nevertheless, we will be at a disadvantage due to this commercial failure. We won't be able to restructure various overhead costs, caused among other things by administrative departments including my Planning department, in step with the decline in production volumes. This means that the costs per employee and tonne produced will increase in comparison to other factories within the production network. We are still hoping for growth in the other product categories, but the latest figures from our monthly planning process do not suggest this will happen soon. In addition, we have been informed that a new network study has been launched to analyse and, if necessary, eliminate overcapacity. Nevertheless, we are all optimistic because our plant covers an extraordinarily large variety of products and thus portfolio complexity. Moreover, we imagine that the large investment sums of the last few years represent a clear commitment to the location.

Before going home, I call Mike. He has known Christoph for several years and has worked with him intensively. I'm interested in how he views him as a line manager, how he behaves and how one ideally works with him. What sticks in my mind from Mike's explanations is that he works in a very unexciting and numbers-oriented way. On a personal level, he seems approachable and fun, yet I should not hope for a mentor or coach in him like Pieter. Especially as a young manager, I find the latter part a pity. Nevertheless, I imagine I can take something away from the future constellation. People in these higher management positions often have some qualities that make them worth learning from.

As we are ending our conversation, Mike asks me if I'm travelling to London next week to take the exams for a supply chain course. Our company has been rolling out an internationally recognised study programme over the last few months and selected managers have been able to take the first courses before this is rolled out to other key employees like my direct reports.

"My exam is on Monday. Sophia and I will fly out early on Saturday to spend the weekend in London."

I still have enough hotel bonus points and air miles, which we are fortunately allowed to use for private purposes.

"Well, have a good time, Gabriel, and I hope you're well prepared."

"Thank you! I think that I've learned enough. I took part in the exam preparation and also worked through the course material on the past weekends. For now, I'm just hoping we have time to relax and enjoy our city trip."

"Why wouldn't you?"

"Well, Sophia likes to make long lists with countless items to tick off during these trips. On Friday night we also have tickets for Paul van Dyk at the O2 Arena in Prague. Depending on what time he's on, we won't get any sleep before going to the airport. Our flight leaves at 7.30 a.m."

"You'll be fine. At least you're never bored with all the challenges at the factory and your private programme."

18 - A Coaching Session

In the last few weeks, a kind of routine has finally set in, which should not be confused with boredom. Christoph's behaviour matches with Mike's portrayal. He also brings a certain calmness to the team. This means that my colleagues and I can work on our initiatives without constantly expecting new escalations and pressure from left and right. Sophia and I took the opportunity to spend a short holiday at Lake Constance. In the meantime, her sister has had a baby and Sophia is now a proud godmother. Back in Prague, I notice that she often seems sad and absent-minded. I can't understand this at all, because we always have a full programme, enjoy our time together and her work also seems to challenge her in a positive sense.

We've just cleared the dining table and now we're planning to have a glass of Spanish red wine and watch a movie. I take the initiative, hold her in my arms and look into her eyes.

"Are you okay?"

"Yes, what could be wrong?"

"Well, since we've been back from your family, you've seemed lost in thoughts."

"You know how important my family is to me and I'm often alone here."

I'm surprised by her direct statement and feel a little attacked at the same time.

"I think I understand but is what we do together not fulfilling enough? We do nice things, like last month's city trips to London, Vienna and Dresden."

"That's true, but I often feel lonely. Watching you I can see how much you're absorbed in your job. You love it. I find it hard to feel the same way. Seeing my little nephew growing up is more important to me than all these trips or sitting next to work colleagues, some of whom don't even make an effort to speak English with me."

"That makes me sad."

"It doesn't have to. I don't want to spoil your mood either."

I still hold her in my arms and press her a little tighter against my chest. I deliberately don't continue the conversation because I have mixed feelings. Sophia is incredibly important to me, but I also realise how much I value my current role at the factory and our life here in the Czech Republic. I promise her that we will visit her family more often and also invite some friends to join us here in Prague. Nevertheless, I'm aware of the sacrifice she makes for me. I love her very much - not only for that.

At the moment, I'm holding individual development discussions with direct reports and talents within my area of responsibility. Right now, I'm sitting with Leos. We are talking about his strengths and weaknesses. We're also drafting a plan for his personal development. What I particularly like is that he also asks me questions. He realises that I'm a fairly young manager and seems to be interested in my career path.

"How come you've already had so many years of professional experience and yet you're so young?"

I laugh and reply, "Well, that's quite simple. I started working before I was eighteen and was always in the right place at the right time afterwards."

"I assume it wasn't quite that simple," he probes.

I take the time to elaborate a little further. I explain to him the German education system and that I left home at the age of sixteen to start an apprenticeship. Explaining further, I emphasise how important on-the-job education is. Especially if you want to become self-employed or pursue a leadership position later on. By studying while you're working, you can further educate yourself – this could be in a specialised subject like logistics or also more general topics like business economics. The combination of professional experience and growing academic and theoretical knowledge constantly creates new perspectives, and one learns to critically question facts and figures. One also gets the appropriate tools and techniques for analysing difficult situations that arise at work. In my case, I did a logistics specialist diploma, followed by the business administration diploma. Along the way, I collected various smaller certificates in project management or became a customs expert. I also explain to Leos that my long-term goal is to obtain an academic degree at a university.

He looks at me in surprise when I share with him how much money and time I've spent on my education so far. He seems to understand that my career was not a pure coincidence and that each of us must pay a certain contribution in order to generate various development opportunities. The saying "success is when preparation meets opportunity" crosses my mind. However, I'm trying to emphasise a completely different point from further training or the constant expansion of knowledge. That is, that in addition to personal flexibility and a willingness to take risks and constantly change, one's personal environment is of the utmost importance.

I tell Leos the story of how, underage and far away from my family, I sought social connection through a local table tennis club. Fortunately, in my club, I met family fathers, business managers, professors and even entrepreneurs who were in the best years of their lives, but also fellow players of the same age as me. In the first few years that I was standing on my own two feet, they greatly influenced me and shared their wisdom and advice after training, over a drink in the clubhouse or during our club's many leisure activities. What was important was not the individual pieces of advice per se, but the way of thinking, the sense of responsibility, the ambition and the motivation that they revealed to me. I realised something similar during my on-the-job education. Here, too, I met people of similar age, sometimes also older, who all had an undeniable motivation in common, continuously developing themselves and generally holding a positive worldview. Leaders at work, such as one's own line manager, can also be "role models'. I summarise it to Leos as the following: "The people you surround yourself with play a vital role that should not be underestimated. Try to put yourself in an environment where you can develop and be yourself. It should include people from whom you can learn and be inspired. If the surrounding doesn't fit, actively seek change. Everyone, at least in the Western world, has the power to choose their environment."

I notice that I enjoy this coaching session and would like to dedicate more time to them in the future. We continue our dialogue for quite a while. Since this is my last appointment of the day, I can easily spend time on it.

19 - Meeting at Head Office

We are holding our routine morning meeting. It usually starts directly after the planners coming back from the daily production meeting. We stand together in our open-plan office and discuss yesterday's production performance, recent changes to the production plan and the reasons for these changes, any customer delivery shortages as well as on-time and in-full supply performance of our suppliers. Also, any other short-term operational challenges are addressed. My mobile phone vibrates. I can see on the display that it's Pieter who is trying to reach me. As we're in the middle of solving a problem, I decline his call. Once the meeting is over, I go out into the corridor to call him back. He gets straight to the point. "Gabriel, book yourself a flight. I want to see you in Switzerland tomorrow. You can travel back the same day". When I ask what it's about, he brushes me off and says I'll find out soon enough. As my day is full of appointments, I waste no further thought on the call. In the evening, I go to bed earlier so that I can catch the 6:00 a.m. flight to Zurich well-rested.

Shortly after 9:00 a.m., I'm already standing in the offices of the global supply chain headquarters. The flight and subsequent direct train from the airport to Schaffhausen were well coordinated. I greet my former colleagues and Mike winks at me from one of the glass telephone booths. Soon, Pieter arrives. He waves at me and indicates that I should accompany him. As I follow him, I smell the freshly smoked cigar. We change floors and enter a small meeting room. The room is quite dark with red painted walls. I look around and see an envelope and a biro lying on the table. I stop, take a deep breath. As I collect my thoughts, I notice that it's obviously only the two of us. Therefore, it can't be about anything HR-related like a dismissal. Otherwise, a colleague from the personnel department would be present. I point towards the envelope.

"What's going on?"

"Please take a seat, Gabriel. Before I explain the reason for your trip, I need you to sign this confidentiality agreement."

Without thinking any further, I take the document out of the envelope. It's a standard form headed "Non-Disclosure Agreement". I read through the text and sign it. In addition to many standard legal phrases, I notice the name of the project: "Edelweiss". It dawns on me what it could be about. In recent years, the names of alpine flowers have been used as project titles for plant restructurings. I look at Pieter and start the conversation.

"Which factory are we closing this time?"

He clearly notices that I've got a cheeky undertone. He pauses for a moment and looks at me seriously. "Yours!"

Boom - that hit home. I start feeling sick as my stomach tightens. I was not prepared for this to happen. After all the investments in our site north of Prague, I assumed that we would rather benefit from a further capacity reduction in the network. Our labour costs are low, we have sufficient space for additional expansion and have made good progress in recent months. Pieter, meanwhile, is sitting right next to me. No grins, no jokes. It is a serious and sincere discussion. He knows how difficult the situation must be for me and takes the time to explain in detail the reasoning behind this decision. He suggests that I speak with the finance director who can talk me through the rough business case before my return flight. Twenty minutes of explanations and counter-questions pass in a flash. I don't think I've been able to retain any of the arguments at all. My head is spinning, and my body still lingers in a slight state of shock. Before Pieter invites me for a coffee, I ask who among my peers in the factory management team has already been informed about the planned site closure.

"Only Christoph. His assignment mission is the task of handling the plant closure. The rest of the team will only be informed a few months from now."

"Why are you telling me so early?"

"You hold a key position. Your team is the centre piece of information flow for the entire factory. We also need your planning skills to validate the relocation plans. You'll be asked to review the relocation project schedule. Among other things, you'll need to calculate the inventory build-up, evaluate the production line performance before and after relocation and also discuss the details of the product relocations with the receiving plants over the coming months."

Normally I'm not at a loss for words and would come up with countless questions, but I simply do not feel ready for it today. Over more than one and a half years, I have put an infinite amount of time and perseverance into the responsibility I've been given at our plant, transformed the team, and finally, we seem to be doing great. In the last few weeks, I've been so proud of what has been achieved so far and the new positive external perception underlines our progress. Well, in the end my secondment was only meant to last three years, but I had the ambition to leave something sustainable behind – to create something, not to tear it down.

The factory has over one hundred years of history; whole families rely on the work there and we are the most important employer in the region. I try to concentrate on not whining any longer and not sinking into self-pity. I'll have to deal with how my colleagues, my team and everyone else affected reacts to the plant closure announcement soon enough. The rest of the day passes swiftly. I sit down with the finance director a little later and half-heartedly listen to the business case presentation.

Soon I leave for Zurich airport. This time I'm not working on the train or the plane. I have my headphones on and get stuck on melancholic music while browsing through my iPod. During the short flight I manage to fall asleep. It's already dark outside as I arrive home. Sophia sees me coming home with my hanging shoulders and a sad face. She comes over to me and gives me a comforting hug. She doesn't ask any questions – I don't feel like talking either, only get a "hello" past my lips. I don't want to speak about what happened until the next morning. Only at the breakfast table do I tell her that we'll probably need to move on in approximately twelve to sixteen months.

Without any guidance on how to deal with the situation or how to behave, I commute to the factory. In the end, I now have two jobs. Job number one: to continue implementing the improvement actions recorded via our scorecard as if nothing happened yesterday. Job number two: to travel fortnightly to meet with the project team and the plant managers of the receiving sites who will take over our products and machines and to work secretly on the hidden agenda of the site closure.

Yesterday Pieter provided me with the possibility of being transferred directly to a new position should I not feel confident managing the task at hand. But I'll call him later and tell him that he can count me in. My decision is mainly based on wanting to be there for my team and my colleagues and help them navigate the upcoming storm. During the night, I played out countless scenarios in my mind. In the end, I always came to the point where I wanted to take responsibility even in this difficult time. I'll accompany my team and the factory through this final negative period; I won't run away. The saying "every crisis is also an opportunity" comes to my mind. There's at least a last spark of hope that we can turn the business case in our favour and possibly find a solution other than the complete closure of our factory. I'm briefly ashamed of wishing our fate upon another factory.

20 - Living a Double Life

There are days when you just want the ground to open up and swallow you. Today is one of those days. When I enter the office, all eyes are on me. I've replayed the situation in my mind several times on the commute to work: Simply wish the team a good morning and carry on – as if nothing unusual happened yesterday. Jana seems to sense that something is different. She looks at me penetratingly but also somehow sympathetically. "Hey Gabriel, what's up? You seem so sad."

"Oh, I just didn't sleep well. Everything is fine. Thanks for asking."

She doesn't buy into what I say, shakes her head and signals that she's there for me if I want to talk.

I feel awful and I'm lacking energy because of a sleepless night. Feeling sick to my stomach, I force myself to eat an apple to calm down a bit. Afterwards, I dive into work to stop the negative thoughts and feelings. During the lunch break, Jana and Magdalena try again to find out what's going on. They ask questions about what happened on the business trip yesterday and whether everything is fine at home with Sophia. I feel touched by their interest, but it only fuels my guilty conscience. I've never liked not being able to be straightforward and honest. Well, they'll find out soon enough what's going on. No need to put such a burden on them for the moment, I reassure myself.

In the evening, I go upstairs to visit Christoph.

"I've been expecting you all day," he says as I knock on his door. "Pieter has informed me that you're now aware of the major project. How are you doing with that?"

I talk in detail about my emotions but also assure him that he can count me in. Christoph has already been in charge of several restructurings at other production sites. He shares some of his experiences with me. We also talk about the next milestones and which tasks we have to prepare in the background over the coming weeks. An important point is also when we'll involve the rest of the management team. Christoph refers to an external meeting that has already been planned to talk through the annual budget planning for the next business year, followed by a small team event like bowling. "Three more months," I whisper to myself. Three months of not telling the truth and working on a hidden agenda. Christoph fully understands my concerns and reassures me that this has always been the most difficult phase for him, too: The phase of secrecy and, above all, of loneliness because you can't express your feelings or worries to anyone at work.

A little later, we get back to more tangible business topics. We review the rough project plan, and with that, I finally realise how fast we're going to shut down the factory. The last production is to take place within less than a year and a half. The big announcement to the workforce is to be made halfway through. Individual production lines are heading for England, Poland and Romania.

I take the opportunity to ask again about the millions of euros invested during recent years. He calmly explains the concept of "sunk costs". Ultimately, past investments are irrelevant for future business decisions. They can no longer be revised and therefore no longer be considered for taking a new business case decision. Furthermore, I see from the discussion that our low personnel costs here in the Czech Republic are, in fact, a disadvantage as the sum of the planned severance payments, compared to plants in France or Spain, is significantly lower, even though we employ more people. That's mainly triggered by strong unions in those countries leading to multiple years of severance obligations in case of reorganisations. Now I better understand individual points that were presented to me yesterday when I met the supply chain finance director.

Finally, we discuss my personal tasks. I'll need to create various scenarios for demand planning, production planning, but also inventory projections. These should outline in detail where and when we must create capacities in order to build up appropriate stocks for the transfer of products and machinery. Since we produce goods with short shelf lives,

I'm also supposed to analyse at what point we would have to check the possibility of shelf-life extensions or whether we can produce elsewhere within the network at another manufacturing site.

I now learn that Mike is also already involved in the project. Therefore, we can align and assess all analyses together - especially in cases that also concern other production locations. My successor in Rotterdam is also involved as this factory is supposed to be part of the solution to bridge the transfer period.

I explain to Christoph that we will have to involve key members of my team quite soon. In the planning department, these inventory build-ups are very transparent and especially if we are to stockpile components or have products produced at other locations, I have to coordinate this with the help of key planners. I get his agreement to include Jana, Leos and Magdalena in the confidentiality circle immediately after fully onboarding the leadership team.

An important point that Mike and I need to review is the scenarios for ramping up transferred lines at the receiving plants. We know that it can take a few months to reach the desired target performance, that is, equipment efficiency, even with an existing machine freshly set up after a move to another location. Further, we definitely need to deep dive into the demand plans. We have a constant change in the product portfolio. Marketing and Sales regularly launch new products or generate a key share of sales via promotions. We'll have to study the forecasts in detail to understand which commercial activities may have to be postponed or cancelled during the transfer period.

I'm glad that we've already made such good progress with our rolling monthly planning concept. I can re-use many templates from the Supply Review for the analysis of our site closure project – the capacity models, especially, will add a lot of value. I imagine for a brief moment what it would be like to do the transfer planning without our already achieved process stabilisation – pure chaos! When I started at the Nelahozeves factory there was hardly a week in which we realised the planned production output and targeted product mix. We were constantly in crisis mode.

Before I call it a day, we plan the next business trips. We will now meet fortnightly with the receiving plants and the project team from headquarters in one of Zurich's large airport hotels. There we will discuss the project progress and I will present updated analyses of demand, supply and inventory planning, among other things. Ultimately, it's a given that this major project must be implemented smoothly and without hiccups to ensure that our external customers do not experience any restrictions in the delivery performance and product availability in the supermarket or at wholesalers.

21 - Breaking the Bad News

I'm ashamed to admit that the last few weeks have been continuously exciting and educational. My initial worries about whether I would be able to cope with the variety of tasks quickly faded. I've started to like the relevance of the analyses and the exchanges with the project management and peers in the other production locations. As time has passed, I've been able to gain a deeper insight into the expected savings and thus understand the business need behind the project. Lost market shares, and therefore, declining sales volumes have led to significant overcapacities at various production sites. Competitors have been able to occupy important points of sale, for example, through successful product innovations, but also clear cost advantages. As a result, consumers in many European markets have been buying and consuming our products less frequently. Investments in new manufacturing technologies are also planned for the coming years. To this end, the machine park must first be streamlined to enable further economies of scale.

In addition, I've gained confidence in the undertaking by being able to recognise a few times how the business case for the plant closure was adjusted based on new findings. This means that no false promises are made to top management. This makes me hope that my colleagues in the management team will find it less difficult to accept the drastic restructuring decision. The project's risk matrix has also been filled to the brim and will contribute to the constant search for optimisations and the successful implementation of the project plan. In the meantime, we have reached the point of no return and we need to disclose the project to the rest of our factory's leadership. We have to get into the deepest details. Decisions on HR topics can no longer be postponed. The final severance package should be agreed, and official applications submitted. The technical details of machine transfers also need to be refined. For this, we need the knowledge of our production manager, Pavel, for example.

Due to the hustle and bustle, I have been able to spend even less free time with Sophia on workdays. The many business trips have also meant that I regularly spend some nights away from home. So far, she seems to be coping well and hasn't complained to me. At least in my thoughts I've not neglected her at all. Deep inside me, an idea is maturing that I would like to reveal during our upcoming family visit to Lake Constance.

Tonight, I'm particularly nervous. Tomorrow is the day we have the planned appointment with the site management team at a hotel in Prague, where we're supposed to discuss next year's financial budget and close the day with a team dinner and bowling. I pour myself a glass of red wine to distract myself and relax a bit. Unfortunately, alcohol seems to have the opposite effect. A walk in the fresh air often helps me when I'm nervous, especially in the evening when it's dark and the streets are empty. Sophia accompanies me and we walk hand in hand through the district of Vokovice. It's comforting to have an empathetic partner by my side in such difficult phases. Stretching the legs works and I'm able to find a few hours of sleep.

The next day I leave the factory after lunch and drive to the seminar hotel. Magdalena calls after me, "Have fun bowling". I wave to her from the open car window and think of the imminent shock for my colleagues. On the way into town, I try to distract myself with loud electronic music.

An hour later, the leadership team meets in the reserved meeting room. The mood is cheerful and most of us pour a cup of coffee before Christoph's intro. Today I prefer to avoid the caffeine. Suddenly, everything is happening way too fast. Even I'm caught off guard with the proceedings and expected to approach the actual topic with small, careful steps. In the end, there is probably no right or wrong way to proceed in such a delicate situation. Sometimes it's better to lay the cards openly on the table and just deal with the emerging reactions. I didn't really hear the first words of our plant manager, "... I have to tell you that an irrevocable and serious decision has been taken. The Nelahozeves factory will be closed down next year at the latest."

The long-service team members look around in disbelief and our technical manager, Jan, who has worked at the site for over thirty years, laughs in confusion and exclaims loudly, "You've got to be kidding!"

"No, unfortunately not. We didn't take this decision easily," Christoph replies calmly.

Jan clenches his fist and hits the table hard. His coffee spills over and when he tries to grab the cup, he burns his hand, giving him one more reason to shout out. Other colleagues like Pavel are quiet and don't say a word. Martin, our controller, struggles with his emotions. When I look into his red eyes, he hastily looks away. I also get triggered by this blatant change of mood. It's difficult to suppress unfolding emotions. With a shaky hand, I nip on a glass of water to somehow distract myself physically. Rather quickly, heated words fly around the room. Pavel wants to know when Christoph had been informed about the decision. He replies calmly and level-headedly the same story he told me the day after my briefing. He also points out that I have already been actively involved in the project for a few weeks and have completed various preliminary tasks. Pavel turns to me disapprovingly. I can't talk and simply shrug my shoulders. Christoph gets a little more formal. He reaches into his briefcase and lays out various papers in front of him. He quietly looks at every one of us for a while. Some stand or walk around the room like caged animals.

"I can vaguely imagine how many thoughts are going through your minds. But I have an important question for every one of you. These documents contain details of a fair severance package. You can accept the proposal and be released of your duties without any obstacles. However, I would clearly prefer to face this difficult undertaking and stick together as a uniform team to shut down the site in the best possible way for all parties involved."

The colleagues are chatting in Czech, so Christoph and I cannot follow. A few minutes later, the team reports back that none of them will resign nor escape this uncomfortable situation. I recognise a fighting spirit and imagine that they must be going through the same emotional rollercoaster that I experienced a while ago. This includes countless business case reviews to see if there were any mistakes or wrong assumptions that may revise the decision.

Christoph nods contentedly to the group and asks whether we still have the energy to discuss the various project phases or whether we should move on to the social part of the day. The answer from Jan, Martin and Pavel is clear. There's no way they are going to pursue any fun activities now. They would rather go home and recover from the shock. Tomorrow is another day to discuss further details, they say. We close the meeting. The team leaves only one hour after the meeting started. It certainly seemed longer to me. At least within the leadership team, we can finally talk openly with each other. The parallel work on the hidden agenda items, along with the daily stressful operational tasks and especially my guilty conscience, have sapped a lot of my energy lately. Unfortunately, over seven hundred people still need to be informed.

22 - Looks Like Team Spirit

It is amazing how one can be motivated even under adverse circumstances. Even though we did not manage to influence the plant restructuring business case in our favour, we have worked well as a unified team so far and invested a lot of energy in optimising various aspects of the project. In addition, we spent a few days with the idea of taking over the plant ourselves, or at least parts of it, in a kind of management buy-out. However, such a business case requires a lot of capital and consequently carries a lot of entrepreneurial risks, so in the end, we couldn't pursue that option any further.

On the positive side, we managed to negotiate a good severance package for our staff. As there are no strong trade unions or workers' representatives in Czech companies, this responsibility was mainly in the hands of the site leadership team. Just a few months ago, another large location not too far away from ours closed down. There the package was the equivalent of approximately one year's salary. We managed to get an even better agreement for our employees. In a nutshell, we're talking about a compensation package worth multiple millions of euros. We put a lot of thought into the payout scheme. In addition to good base compensation, we also wanted to link a not insignificant part of the severance pay to various performance targets during the final phase of the plant closure. For example, another two months of severance pay will be released if certain production fulfilment levels are reached. Employees who remain on-site until the bitter end or who ensure that the relocated manufacturing lines are properly handed over and ramped up can realise further payouts. It has also been checked whether there are relatives like spouses among the staff members. If so, solutions are sought to release at least one of the partners at a later date as they will be entitled to higher compensation.

These small things within our area of influence motivate us as leaders. Personally, this has also helped my morale whilst dealing with the crisis. For key members of my administrative team, like Jana and Magdalena, I'm trying to create job opportunities within the company beyond plant closure. For this purpose, with the employees' consent, I've created an overview with relevant milestones of their curriculum vitae as well as strengths and development potential. Fortunately, I'm well connected, knowing several plant managers and supply chain managers of the various markets. I approach my network to look for transfer opportunities for the most capable employees.

The team leaders like Jana and Magdalena, as well as Leos in his function as key production planner, are now also familiar with the project. They are dealing with it much better than expected. It was also interesting that Jana could tell me exactly when I had been informed about the factory closure. She could directly recall when I came back from the business trip to Switzerland with a sad face a couple of months ago.

Also, the company has already offered me a new position. Next year, I can take over from a colleague who is retiring. It's a central but highly specialised supply chain role. To be honest, I'd like to continue working as a member of a site management team, but for Sophia s sake, we'll return to Switzerland or southern Germany. Due to the move to Prague, my plans for further training have been on hold for a while now. Therefore, as part of the new employment contract, I agreed that I would be sponsored to study on the job for a Master of Business Administration. It has always been my dream to obtain an academic degree, even without a high school certificate. However, there are still challenging months ahead, so after agreeing on the details of the contract, I won't spend any further thought on this role for the moment. Here at the site, my attention and energy are still needed, and I don t want to be distracted. Moreover, I am in no hurry to leave the Czech Republic. If I were single, I could even imagine staying for longer and, if necessary, changing companies, even for a locally adjusted income.

We are currently receiving support from an occupational psychologist. With her help, we prepare for the announcement and other personnel-related activities. We study how to deal with critical situations and deepen what we have learned in role plays. We also touch on legal aspects and the entitlement and formalities for unemployment benefits and the like. We want to be well prepared when we face overwhelmed staff members. Above all, we want to avoid further disadvantages for them, for example, because formal application deadlines are missed.

I won't be bored, that's certain. Some of our special products cannot be relocated within the existing production network. For this, our procurement department is currently looking for potential contract manufacturers. Next week, Magdalena and I will travel to Austria to meet one of these.

Sophia has started looking for a new employment contract as well. I'm curious to know when and where she will find a new job. I'm a little worried that she will succeed too soon, and we will be separated for several months. When looking in the mirror in the morning, the mental but also the emotional stress of the last few weeks is clearly visible. Dark circles under my eyes are noticeable and I'm often exhausted in the evenings and therefore don't do as much sport. It's a vicious cycle and I'm fighting it by being more disciplined.

Our upcoming short holiday comes at a good time. Next week we're going to visit Sophia's family in Constance. Among other things, Sophia will have a job interview there as well. Most of the time, however, will be spent visiting family or friends and in a hopefully relaxing atmosphere. We will also start searching for a new apartment, so we've planned the first viewings. This way, we can possibly sign a contract for our new home to ensure a smoother departure from the Czech Republic and minimise potential trouble. Since the big announcement is coming soon, this will be the last holiday before the hot phase of the project.

23 – Message in a Bottle

It's Saturday evening. Sophia and I are walking in the twilight in the middle of Constance along the lake. We've already met up with good friends in the afternoon and booked a table at the steakhouse for dinner. A few minutes ago, I came up with an excuse that I'd forgotten something in the car and therefore had to go back to the car park. I ask our friends to wait for me with Sophia. In fact, I have to go back to the car because I've prepared something. I open the boot and grab what I need. On my way back, I take a short detour to be able to place a surprise along our route. I hurry and walk swiftly back to the others. My hands start sweating, and I notice my heartbeat, not just because of my haste.

A little later as we walk along the promenade I point towards the water and ask Sophia if she also sees something floating there. We walk a little closer to the object and recognise it's a bottle. I point to a string wedged under a stone nearby us. Sophia pulls the bottle out of the water. She sees the message in the bottle and unscrews the cap. The string is also attached to the letter, so she can easily pull it out. My face turns red because of the excitement, but fortunately it's not that visible during twilight. Sophia becomes quiet as she reads the letter. It starts with how happy she makes me. I thank her for her unconditional support over the past years and pay her various compliments. During our time in Prague, a decision has matured in me: I want to spend my life with Sophia.

While she continues reading, my thoughts wander. I remember a summer holiday six years ago. A good friend and I travelled from southern Germany to Sweden, then on to the island of Rügen and last but not least, we stayed a few days in Berlin. During our men's holiday, I annoyed him so much by going on and on about Sophia, who I had just met shortly before, that we invited her to Berlin at short notice. Luckily, she accepted and joined us. One summer evening later, she strolled barefoot next to me through Berlin. This is where we held hands for the first time and officially became a couple. I remember very clearly how excited and in love I was - that's exactly how I feel again right now.

When she finishes reading and looks over, I get down on my knees and ask, "Will you marry me?" By now our friends are as thrilled as I am. Without much hesitation, she answers, "Yes". She asks me to get up, hugs and kisses me. Beaming with joy and holding hands, we move on towards the restaurant.

24 - The Big Day

We are currently clearing one of our on-site raw material warehouses. The reasoning behind this is rather vague and I told the team it's about a bigger maintenance measure. The empty warehouse will provide us with sufficient space to conduct the long-planned announcement next week. It has been planned to split the audience into two groups. In the morning, we'll start with the day shift and office staff. In the evening, we'll inform the remaining shifts about the plant's future. By now, I've turned into a seasoned crisis manager and my usually overbooked agenda leaves little room for fantasies. Nevertheless, one can feel the crackling tension in the air.

In the meantime, there have been some rumours among the staff, which we have so far denied. Together with the Corporate Communications department, we have prepared "holding statements". These contain clear instructions on how we should react to internal but also external enquiries related to the project. Above all, it is important not to spread lies but to provide answers that do not carry too much weight. I often feel like a politician who is just talking in platitudes. In such a late project phase, rumours are almost impossible to prevent. Especially the constant involvement of suppliers and other external project partners makes it difficult to keep control over all communications or even misdirected enquiries.

It is the evening before the big day. At home, I'm rehearsing tomorrow's schedule. Suddenly my mobile phone vibrates. Leos has sent me a text message: "Hi Gabriel, check your e-mails. I sent a link to an article from a local news corporation." I open his e-mail and click on the link. It takes me to the website of a Prague newspaper. I copy the text into a language programme to have it translated into German. I develop weak knees and ask Sophia to come over. We read the text together, which claims that my company will close the production site in Nelahozeves and that over seven hundred employees will be laid off. I call Christoph and inform him about the incident. He is already informed. After reassuring me, he points out that we will stick to our communication plan without any change. This event will not help me to fall asleep faster.

The next morning, I force myself to have some breakfast. The day will be eventful, and I'll need sufficient energy. Sophia almost has to throw me out of our flat. Mixed emotions overcome me, and thus, I need more time than usual for my morning routine. During the commute to the factory, I cannot get a calm mind. I think about the news from last night and how the staff will react. A French colleague had told me about an experience where he and the rest of the factory management were locked up on-site for several days in a similar situation. I remain confident because so far, the employees who have been informed have reacted calmly and respectfully. There is nothing to reproach the site leadership team with, as we have worked hard to get the best out of the tricky situation, despite no happy end.

When I reach the factory, everything is normal. There are no unusual occurrences at the security check. I drive onto the factory premises and park my car.

An hour later, I'm at the allocated warehouse with about four hundred people. Christoph, the main speaker, is holding the microphone. Next to him, there is a senior executive from the Czech head office who will act as an interpreter. The management team, including myself, is lined up in front of the many rows of seats. You can literally feel the tension – it is surprisingly quiet even though so many people are gathered. Christoph welcomes the staff, and after each sentence, he pauses for translation.

I have heard the speech several times before, but this time there is something definitive about it. I'm nervous, especially as I'll have to deal with questions and comments from my fifty-plus staff after the general announcement. Nevertheless, I lose a heavy burden because everything is finally in the open, and we can react actively and honestly to any upcoming events. Christoph has meanwhile said the pivotal sentence. When the date of the last production is mentioned, I see shocked faces all over the room. I think hardly anyone could have imagined that we would be able to shut down such a large site within a few months. Tears flow. Individual employees fall into one another's arms and encourage each other. There is no aggression or loud interjections.

Next, our human resources manager takes the stage and explains the rest of today's schedule. He explains where each department will meet and indicates that all supervisors will reveal further details and take time to answer any questions. The management team stays in the warehouse and waits until the ranks have thinned out. Christoph pats some of us on the back encouragingly. Then we go to our teams.

The meeting with the warehouse staff goes without excitement. There are a few questions. First and foremost, they ask about the severance pay, then how long each production line will remain in operation and how we intend to reduce staffing over the coming months. The colleague from the human resources department, who has joined for support, explains to the team once again the formalities for filing for unemployment and that we will provide each employee with application training and other help such as outplacement.

The interview with the administrative staff is way more demanding. I'm literally showered with questions. It's immediately noticeable that team members below the age of thirty have few concerns about their future. They are more interested in the why and also want to understand the business case for the site closure. They ask many legitimate and critical questions. Thanks to the good preparation and the many detailed analyses in which I was, for the most part, personally involved, I'm able to answer many of the questions satisfactorily.

This feels like the longest and most emotionally exhausting day of my career so far. We still have to conduct the second round of the announcement in the late evening. Of course, the participants have already been pre-informed in detail by the colleagues who participated in the morning session, so it turns out fewer questions are asked, and the emotions are not as dramatic.

Around midnight I finally return home. I'm exhausted and fall asleep as soon as I hit the bed.

25 - That's Business

The very next day, the large glass filling line is dismantled. A huge crane lifts it out of the production building. The production line was moved to us from the Netherlands just two years ago. Now it's going to be relocated once more – this time heading for London. A few experienced crew members will a little later accompany the filling line for several months to ensure a smooth rebuild and ramp-up in England.

With astonishing speed, the lines go down, one after another and some are transferred as well. Many of our finished products are reallocated to other plants or the selected contract manufacturers. The ranks of the workforce thin out over time. Truly amazing is the fact that we have not lost a single production hour due to disagreements or industrial action. Staff have commented several times that we offered a fair and balanced severance package. So, even in these challenging circumstances, we have received unexpected kudos from the workforce.

This difficult phase, from the preparation to the gradual closure of our factory, has impacted me intensely. I'm infinitely grateful to my colleagues for the respectful, positive interactions and fair dialogues. I find the numerous farewells particularly difficult, especially amongst the blue-collar workers.

There are various older team members in my area of responsibility who are not well educated and have never worked elsewhere than our factory. I fervently hope that they will make ends meet with the help of the severance payment and hopefully find a job sooner rather than later.

What fills me with pride is that my efforts to transfer talented planners have paid off. We were able to find Magdalena a job at our company's head office in Prague. Jana has been offered an international project role. I'm extraordinarily happy for Leos. He will move internationally to become a production planner in another factory. His teammate, the lateral entrant who took Ondrej's position with, is also moving to another plant in Germany.

There are only six weeks left until the very last production. Sophia is already living in our new flat in southern Germany, and I'm back at the Hilton, where it all started. The move from the Czech Republic to Germany went just as smoothly and professionally as last time. Today I have to hand in my company car and Marek will take me to the airport one last time. Until now, I had not longed for the day of my departure from the Czech Republic. But without Sophia, Prague city life was less fun and at work, too, my beloved team was steadily decimated. It's quite depressing to see this once great and vibrant factory being shut down. Without a doubt, it's time to leave with good memories and to start looking forward to new ventures. It has been the most formative experience of my career so far, with successes, failures, sweat and tears, but also a lot of fun. I'll miss the vibrant city of Prague, especially my teammates.

There is a last knock on my door. It's Marek.

"Are you ready?" he asks in broken German.

I nod. Nobody is in the office anymore, the remaining colleagues called it a day and I've already said goodbye. Marek accompanies me to the site security, where I hand in my access card and car key. I step onto the factory grounds for one last time, turn around and memorise the silhouettes of the buildings. With a mixture of sadness, pride and confidence, I get into Marek's car, and we set off. In the side mirror I thoughtfully watch the factory getting smaller and smaller until it finally disappears.

The Author

Martin Hendel, born in 1982, is a father of three children and lives with his wife in Germany. He has two decades of practical experience in supply chain management.

Martin acquired, applied and deepened his knowledge with renowned employers in the consumer goods industry, such as Unilever and Carlsberg. In addition to Germany and Switzerland, he had the opportunity to work in large production facilities in the Netherlands and the Czech Republic as a member of the site management team (Head of Logistics, Head of Supply Chain Planning/Management). He was also responsible for implementing significant supply chain process and planning systems at various European manufacturing plants.

He currently works in the healthcare industry and holds the position of Vice President, Supply Chain Planning at Paul Hartmann AG in Heidenheim, Germany.

As an enthusiastic leader, Martin is constantly looking for improvements and optimisation potential. He is involved as an Enabler in "Startup Netzwerk Bodensee" and, through this platform and with his diverse expertise and experience, he tries to support new, regional companies to move forward.

Martin embodies lifelong learning. He is a trained forwarding merchant, logistics specialist, business economist and holds a Master's degree in Business Administration.

You can contact him via:

- Website https://deine-lieferkette.de (German content),
- YouTube channel "Supply Chain College" (German content)
- Common Podcast platforms under "Supply Chain College" (German content), or
- LinkedIn.

Thanks to my parents, who have always believed in and supported me. To my wife Ricarda and our three children for their patience and many freedoms. To my companions, especially Andreas and Timo, for their friendship, and my former and current colleagues for all the learning opportunities and constant feedback!

If you enjoyed reading the book and found valuable content, I would appreciate a personal review on Amazon. Thank you for being so helpful!

Printed in Great Britain
by Amazon

42843830R00108